READY NOTES AND SOLUTIONS TO ODD-NUMBERED PROBLEMS

for use with

ACCOUNTING
WHAT THE NUMBERS MEAN

Third Edition

David H. Marshall
Professor Emeritus of Accounting
Millikin University
Wayne W. McManus
University of Missouri–Kansas City

Boston, Massachusetts Burr Ridge, Illinios Dubuque, Iowa
Madison, Wisconsin New York, New York San Francisco, California St. Louis, Missouri

Irwin/McGraw-Hill

A Division of The ***McGraw·Hill*** *Companies*

Printed in the United States of America.

ISBN 0-256-21596-0

6 7 8 9 0 QPD 2 1 0 9 8 7

Contents

SOLUTIONS TO ODD-NUMBERED PROBLEMS

ACCOUNTING IS THE PROCESS OF:

IDENTIFYING >
MEASURING >
COMMUNICATING >

ECONOMIC INFORMATION ABOUT AN ENTITY FOR

> DECISIONS
> INFORMED JUDGMENTS

USERS OF ACCOUNTING INFORMATION

MANAGEMENT

INVESTORS

CREDITORS

EMPLOYEES

GOVERNMENTAL AGENCIES

CLASSIFICATIONS OF ACCOUNTING

FINANCIAL ACCOUNTING

MANAGERIAL ACCOUNTING / COST ACCOUNTING

AUDITING - PUBLIC / INTERNAL

GOVERNMENTAL ACCOUNTING

INCOME TAX ACCOUNTING

PROFESSIONAL DEGREES

CPA - CERTIFIED PUBLIC ACCOUNTANT

CMA - CERTIFIED MANAGEMENT ACCOUNTANT

CIA - CERTIFIED INTERNAL AUDITOR

FINANCIAL ACCOUNTING STANDARD SETTING

FASB (FINANCIAL ACCOUNTING STANDARDS BOARD)

> *STATEMENTS OF FINANCIAL ACCOUNTING STANDARDS*
OVER 100 ISSUED. DEAL WITH SPECIFIC ACCOUNTING / REPORTING ISSUES.

> *STATEMENTS OF FINANCIAL ACCOUNTING CONCEPTS*
6 ISSUED. AN ATTEMPT TO PROVIDE A COMMON FOUNDATION TO SUPPORT FINANCIAL ACCOUNTING STANDARDS.

> **KEY OBJECTIVES OF FINANCIAL REPORTING (SFAC #1)**

> RELATE TO EXTERNAL FINANCIAL REPORTING.

> TO SUPPORT BUSINESS AND ECONOMIC DECISIONS.

> TO PROVIDE INFORMATION ABOUT CASH FLOWS.

> PRIMARY FOCUS IS ON EARNINGS BASED ON ACCRUAL ACCOUNTING.

> NOT TO MEASURE DIRECTLY THE VALUE OF A BUSINESS ENTERPRISE.

> INFORMATION REPORTED SUBJECT TO EVALUATION BY INDIVIDUAL FINANCIAL STATEMENT USERS.

> ACCOUNTING STANDARDS ARE STILL EVOLVING.

INTERNATIONAL ACCOUNTING STANDARDS

> IASC (INTERNATIONAL ACCOUNTING STANDARDS COMMITTEE).

> STANDARDS DIFFER SIGNIFICANTLY AMONG COUNTRIES.

> INDIVIDUAL COUNTRY STANDARDS REFLECT LOCAL MARKET NEEDS AND COUNTRY REGULATION AND TAXATION PRACTICES.

ETHICS AND THE ACCOUNTING PROFESSION

> AICPA CODE OF PROFESSIONAL CONDUCT

> IMA STANDARDS OF ETHICAL CONDUCT FOR MANAGEMENT ACCOUNTANTS

KEY ELEMENTS OF ETHICAL BEHAVIOR

> INTEGRITY

> OBJECTIVITY

> INDEPENDENCE

> COMPETENCE

TRANSACTIONS TO FINANCIAL STATEMENTS

TRANSACTIONS > PROCEDURES FOR SORTING, CLASSIFYING AND PRESENTING (BOOKKEEPING). SELECTION OF ALTERNATIVE METHODS OF REFLECTING THE THE EFFECTS OF TRANSACTIONS (ACCOUNTING). > FINANCIAL STATEMENTS

TRANSACTIONS

> ECONOMIC INTERCHANGES BETWEEN ENTITIES.

EXAMPLES:

FINANCIAL STATEMENTS

> **BALANCE SHEET**
FINANCIAL POSITION AT A POINT IN TIME.

> **INCOME STATEMENT**
EARNINGS FOR A PERIOD OF TIME.

> **STATEMENT OF CASH FLOWS**
SUMMARY OF CASH FLOWS FOR A PERIOD OF TIME.

> **STATEMENT OF CHANGES IN OWNERS' EQUITY**
INVESTMENTS BY OWNERS, EARNINGS OF THE FIRM, AND DISTRIBUTIONS TO OWNERS FOR A PERIOD OF TIME.

FINANCIAL STATEMENTS

BALANCE SHEET (AT A POINT IN TIME)

EXHIBIT 2–1 Balance Sheet

MAIN STREET STORE, INC.
Balance Sheet
August 31, 1996

Assets		Liabilities and Owners' Equity	
Current assets:		Current liabilities:	
Cash	$ 34,000	Short-term debt	$ 20,000
Accounts receivable	80,000	Accounts payable	35,000
Merchandise inventory	170,000	Other accrued liabilities	12,000
Total current assets	$284,000	Total current liabilities	$ 67,000
Plant and equipment:			
Equipment	40,000	Long-term debt	50,000
Less: Accumulated depreciation	(4,000)	Total liabilities	$117,000
		Owners' equity	203,000
Total assets	$320,000	Total liabilities and owners' equity	$320,000

KEY RELATIONSHIP

ASSETS = LIABILITIES + OWNERS' EQUITY

KEY TERMINOLOGY

> ASSETS

> CURRENT ASSETS

> ACCUMULATED DEPRECIATION

> LIABILITIES

> CURRENT LIABILITIES

> OWNERS' EQUITY

FINANCIAL STATEMENTS

INCOME STATEMENT (FOR A PERIOD OF TIME)

EXHIBIT 2–2 Income Statement

MAIN STREET STORE, INC.
Income Statement
For the Year Ended August 31, 1996

Net Sales	$1,200,000
Cost of goods sold	850,000
Gross profit	$ 350,000
Selling, general, and administrative expenses	311,000
Earnings from operations	$ 39,000
Interest expense	9,000
Earnings before taxes	$ 30,000
Income taxes	12,000
Net income	$ 18,000
Net income per share of common stock outstanding	$ 1.80

KEY RELATIONSHIP

REVENUES - EXPENSES = NET INCOME

KEY TERMINOLOGY

> REVENUES (SALES)

> COST OF GOODS SOLD

> GROSS PROFIT

> OPERATING INCOME

> EARNINGS BEFORE TAXES

> NET INCOME

> NET INCOME PER SHARE OF COMMON STOCK

FINANCIAL STATEMENTS

STATEMENT OF CHANGES IN OWNERS' EQUITY
(FOR A PERIOD OF TIME)

EXHIBIT 2–3 Statement of Changes in Owners' Equity

MAIN STREET STORE, INC.
Statement of Changes in Owners' Equity
For the Year Ended August 31, 1996

Paid-in capital:	
Beginning balance.	$ –0–
Common stock, par value, $10; 50,000 shares authorized, 10,000 shares issued and outstanding	100,000
Additional paid-in capital	90,000
Balance, August 31, 1996	$190,000
Retained earnings:	
Beginning balance.	$ –0–
Net income for the year	18,000
Less: Cash dividends of $.50 per share	(5,000)
Balance, August 31, 1996	$ 13,000
Total owners' equity	$203,000

TWO PRINCIPAL COMPONENTS

> PAID-IN CAPITAL CHANGES

> RETAINED EARNINGS CHANGES

KEY RELATIONSHIP

RETAINED EARNINGS BEGINNING BALANCE
\+ NET INCOME FOR THE PERIOD
\- DIVIDENDS
= RETAINED EARNINGS ENDING BALANCE

KEY TERMINOLOGY

> PAID-IN CAPITAL   > DIVIDENDS

FINANCIAL STATEMENTS

STATEMENT OF CASH FLOWS (FOR A PERIOD OF TIME)

EXHIBIT 2–4 Statement of Cash Flows

MAIN STREET STORE, INC.
Statement of Cash Flows
For the Year Ended August 31, 1996

Cash flows from operating activities:	
Net income	$ 18,000
Add (deduct) items not affecting cash:	
Depreciation expense	4,000
Increase in accounts receivable	(80,000)
Increase in merchandise inventory	(170,000)
Increase in current liabilities	67,000
Net cash used by operating activities	$(161,000)
Cash flows from investing activities:	
Cash paid for equipment	$ (40,000)
Cash flows from financing activities:	
Cash received from issue of long-term debt	$ 50,000
Cash received from sale of common stock	190,000
Payment of cash dividend on common stock	(5,000)
Net cash provided by financing activities	$ 235,000
Net increase in cash for the year	$ 34,000

KEY TERMINOLOGY

> CASH FLOWS FROM OPERATING ACTIVITIES

> CASH FLOWS FROM INVESTING ACTIVITIES

> CASH FLOWS FROM FINANCING ACTIVITIES

> CHANGE IN CASH FOR THE YEAR

FINANCIAL STATEMENT RELATIONSHIPS

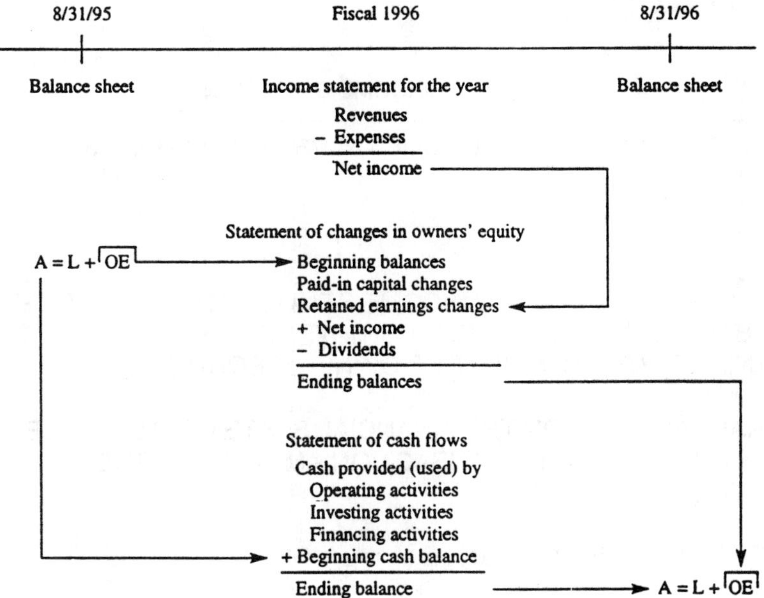

KEY IDEAS

> TRANSACTIONS AFFECTING THE INCOME STATEMENT ALSO AFFECT THE BALANCE SHEET.

> FOR THE BALANCE SHEET TO BALANCE, INCOME STATEMENT TRANSACTIONS MUST BE REFLECTED IN THE RETAINED EARNINGS PART OF OWNERS' EQUITY.

> THE STATEMENT OF CASH FLOWS EXPLAINS WHY THE CASH AMOUNT CHANGED DURING THE PERIOD.

A MODEL OF THE RELATIONSHIP BETWEEN THE BALANCE SHEET AND INCOME STATEMENT

BALANCE SHEET		INCOME STATEMENT
ASSETS = LIABILITIES + OWNERS' EQUITY	<	NET INCOME = REVENUES - EXPENSES

KEY IDEAS

> THE ARROW FROM NET INCOME IN THE INCOME STATEMENT TO OWNERS' EQUITY IN THE BALANCE SHEET INDICATES THAT NET INCOME AFFECTS RETAINED EARNINGS, WHICH IS PART OF OWNERS' EQUITY.

> THE EFFECT OF TRANSACTIONS ON THE FINANCIAL STATEMENTS CAN BE ILLUSTRATED BY ENTERING THE TRANSACTION AMOUNTS IN THE APPROPRIATE COLUMNS.

> THE BALANCE SHEET MUST BE IN BALANCE (A = L + OE) AFTER EVERY TRANSACTION.

ACCOUNTING CONCEPTS AND PRINCIPLES

ACCOUNTING ENTITY

ASSETS = LIABILITIES + OWNERS' EQUITY (ACCOUNTING EQUATION)

GOING CONCERN (CONTINUITY)

TRANSACTIONS > PROCEDURES FOR SORTING, CLASSIFYING AND PRESENTING (BOOKKEEPING) / SELECTION OF ALTERNATIVE METHODS OF REFLECTING THE EFFECTS OF TRANSACTIONS (ACCOUNTING) > FINANCIAL STATEMENTS

UNIT OF MEASUREMENT	ACCOUNTING PERIOD	CONSISTENCY
COST PRINCIPLE	MATCHING REVENUE AND EXPENSE	FULL DISCLOSURE
OBJECTIVITY	REVENUE RECOGNIZED AT TIME OF SALE	MATERIALITY
	ACCRUAL CONCEPT	CONSERVATISM

KEY CLARIFICATION

> MATCHING OF REVENUE AND EXPENSE MEANS THAT ALL EXPENSES INCURRED IN GENERATING REVENUE FOR THE PERIOD ARE SUBTRACTED FROM THOSE REVENUES TO DETERMINE NET INCOME. MATCHING DOES NOT MEAN THAT REVENUES EQUAL EXPENSES.

MEASUREMENTS AND TREND ANALYSIS

PAT'S GPA LAST SEMESTER: 2.8

JUDGMENT SO WHAT? HOW WELL HAS PAT PERFORMED?

PAT'S GPA FOR THE LAST FOUR SEMESTERS:
1.9, 2.3, 2.6, 2.8

JUDGMENT PAT'S PERFORMANCE HAS BEEN IMPROVING.

GPA FOR ALL STUDENTS FOR LAST FOUR SEMESTERS:
2.85, 2.76, 2.70, 2.65

JUDGMENT PAT'S PERFORMANCE HAS IMPROVED WHILE PERFORMANCE OF ALL STUDENTS HAS DECLINED.

KEY POINTS

> THE TREND OF DATA IS FREQUENTLY MORE SIGNIFICANT THAN THE DATA ITSELF.

> COMPARISON OF INDIVIDUAL AND GROUP TRENDS IS IMPORTANT WHEN MAKING JUDGMENTS.

RETURN ON INVESTMENT

RATE OF RETURN (**ROI**)

$$\text{RATE OF RETURN} = \frac{\text{AMOUNT OF RETURN}}{\text{AMOUNT INVESTED}}$$

KEY POINTS

> RATE OF RETURN IS AN ANNUAL PERCENTAGE RATE UNLESS OTHERWISE SPECIFIED, THEREFORE

> THE AMOUNT OF RETURN IS THE AMOUNT RECEIVED DURING THE YEAR, AND

> THE AMOUNT INVESTED IS THE AVERAGE AMOUNT INVESTED DURING THE YEAR.

> **ROI IS A SIGNIFICANT MEASURE OF ECONOMIC PERFORMANCE BECAUSE IT DESCRIBES THE RESULTS OBTAINED BY MANAGEMENT'S USE OF THE ASSETS MADE AVAILABLE FOR INVESTMENT DURING THE YEAR.**

THE DUPONT MODEL FOR CALCULATING ROI

$$ROI = MARGIN * TURNOVER$$

$$= \frac{\text{NET INCOME}}{\text{SALES}} * \frac{\text{SALES}}{\text{AVERAGE TOTAL ASSETS}}$$

KEY IDEAS

> MARGIN DESCRIBES THE PROFITABILITY FROM SALES.

> TURNOVER DESCRIBES THE EFFICIENCY WITH WHICH ASSETS HAVE BEEN USED TO GENERATE SALES.

> OVERALL PROFITABILITY - RETURN ON INVESTMENT - IS A FUNCTION OF BOTH PROFITABILITY OF SALES AND THE EFFICIENT USE OF ASSETS.

KEY POINTS

> NET INCOME AND SALES ARE FOR THE YEAR. FOR CONSISTENCY, TOTAL ASSETS IS THE AVERAGE OF TOTAL ASSETS FROM THE BALANCE SHEETS AT THE BEGINNING AND END OF THE YEAR.

> OPERATING INCOME MAY BE USED IN THE MARGIN CALCULATION INSTEAD OF NET INCOME, AND AVERAGE OPERATING ASSETS OR AVERAGE GROSS ASSETS MAY BE USED IN THE TURNOVER CALCULATION. AS LONG AS THE DATA USED ARE CONSISTENTLY CALCULATED, THE TREND OF ROI WILL BE USEFUL FOR JUDGMENTS.

RETURN ON EQUITY (ROE)

$$\text{RETURN ON EQUITY} = \frac{\text{NET INCOME}}{\text{AVERAGE OWNERS' EQUITY}}$$

KEY POINT

> AS IN ROI, NET INCOME IS FOR THE YEAR, THEREFORE IT IS RELATED TO THE AVERAGE OF THE OWNERS' EQUITY AT THE BEGINNING AND END OF THE YEAR.

KEY IDEAS

> ROI RELATES NET INCOME TO AVERAGE TOTAL ASSETS, AND EXPRESSES A RATE OF RETURN ON THE ASSETS USED BY THE FIRM.

> ROE RELATES NET INCOME TO AVERAGE OWNERS' EQUITY, AND EXPRESSES A RATE OF RETURN ON THAT PORTION OF THE ASSETS PROVIDED BY THE OWNERS OF THE FIRM.

WORKING CAPITAL AND MEASURES OF LIQUIDITY

WORKING CAPITAL

CURRENT ASSETS
- CURRENT LIABILITIES
= WORKING CAPITAL

KEY DEFINITIONS

> CURRENT ASSETS: CASH AND ASSETS LIKELY TO BE CONVERTED TO CASH WITHIN A YEAR.

> CURRENT LIABILITIES: OBLIGATIONS THAT MUST BE PAID WITHIN A YEAR.

KEY IDEA

> A MEASURE OF THE FIRM'S ABILITY TO PAY ITS CURRENT OBLIGATIONS.

CURRENT RATIO

$$\frac{\text{CURRENT ASSETS}}{\text{CURRENT LIABILITIES}} = \text{CURRENT RATIO}$$

KEY IDEA

> THE CURRENT RATIO IS USUALLY A MORE USEFUL MEASUREMENT THAN THE AMOUNT OF WORKING CAPITAL BECAUSE IT IS A RATIO MEASUREMENT.

WORKING CAPITAL AND MEASURES OF LIQUIDITY

ACID-TEST RATIO

$$\frac{\text{CASH (INCLUDING TEMPORARY CASH INVESTMENTS) + ACCOUNTS RECEIVABLE}}{\text{CURRENT LIABILITIES}}$$

KEY IDEA

> FOCUSING ON CASH AND ACCOUNTS RECEIVABLE PROVIDES A MORE SHORT-TERM MEASURE OF LIQUIDITY THAN THE CURRENT RATIO.

VERTICAL GRAPH SCALES

ARITHMETIC SCALE

KEY FEATURE

VERTICAL SCALE DISTANCES ARE EQUAL.

KEY IDEA

A CONSTANT RATE OF GROWTH PLOTS AS AN INCREASINGLY STEEP LINE OVER TIME.

LOGARITHMIC SCALE

KEY FEATURE

VERTICAL SCALE DISTANCES ARE INCREASINGLY NARROW AND COMPRESSED.

KEY IDEA

A CONSTANT RATE OF GROWTH PLOTS AS A STRAIGHT LINE.

KEY OBSERVATIONS

> THE HORIZONTAL SCALE WILL ALMOST ALWAYS BE AN ARITHMETIC SCALE, WITH EQUAL DISTANCE BETWEEN THE DATES OF DATA OBSERVATIONS.

> SEMI-LOGARITHMIC FORMAT MEANS THAT THE ONLY THE VERTICAL SCALE IS LOGARITHMIC; THE HORIZONTAL SCALE IS ARITHMETIC.

ARITHMETIC AND SEMI-LOGARITHMIC PLOTS

ARITHMETIC PLOT

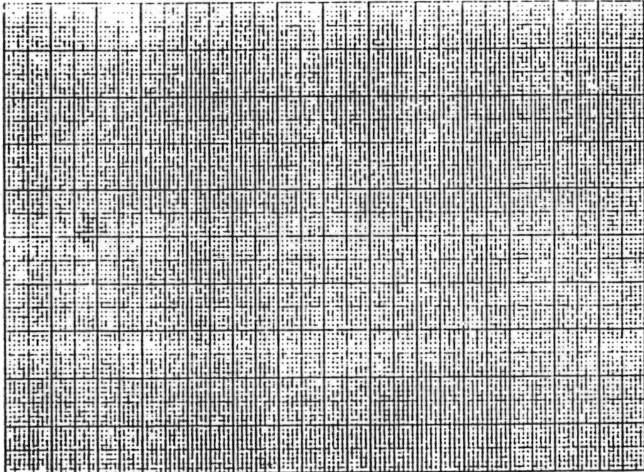

SEMI-LOGARITHMIC PLOT

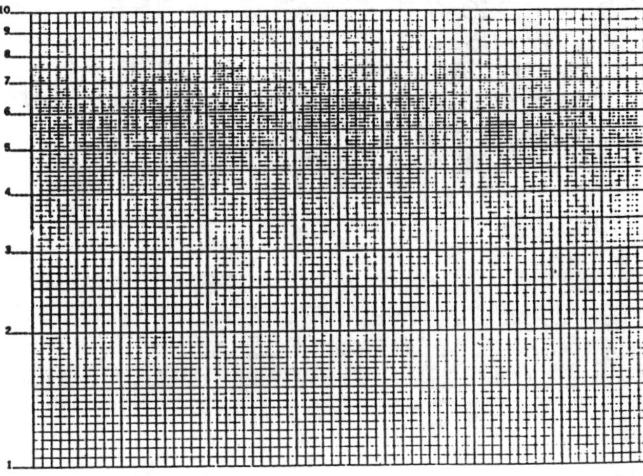

TRANSACTIONS AND THE FINANCIAL STATEMENTS

KEY IDEAS

> > TRANSACTIONS AFFECT THE BALANCE SHEET AND/OR THE INCOME STATEMENT.

> THE BALANCE SHEET MUST BE IN BALANCE AFTER EVERY TRANSACTION.

> THE RETAINED EARNINGS ACCOUNT ON THE BALANCE SHEET INCLUDES NET INCOME FROM THE INCOME STATEMENT.

> BALANCE SHEET ACCOUNTS MAY HAVE AMOUNT BALANCES AT THE END OF A FISCAL PERIOD, AND BEFORE TRANSACTIONS OF THE SUBSEQUENT PERIOD ARE RECORDED.

KEY TERMINOLOGY

> EACH INDIVIDUAL ASSET, LIABILITY, OWNERS' EQUITY, REVENUE, OR EXPENSE "ACCOUNT" MAY ADDITIONALLY BE DESCRIBED WITH ITS CATEGORY TITLE. EXAMPLES:

"CASH ASSET ACCOUNT"
"ACCOUNTS PAYABLE LIABILITY ACCOUNT"
"COMMON STOCK OWNERS' EQUITY ACCOUNT"
"SALES REVENUE ACCOUNT"
"WAGES EXPENSE ACCOUNT"

KEY RELATIONSHIP

> TRANSACTIONS DURING A FISCAL PERIOD CAUSE THE BALANCE OF THE AFFECTED ACCOUNT(S) TO INCREASE OR DECREASE. BOOKKEEPING IS THE PROCESS OF KEEPING TRACK OF THESE CHANGES.

BOOKKEEPING PROCEDURES

WHAT THE BOOKS ARE CALLED

> THE **JOURNAL** IS A CHRONOLOGICAL RECORD OF EACH TRANSACTION.

> THE **LEDGER** IS A BOOK OF ALL OF THE ACCOUNTS: ACCOUNTS ARE USUALLY ARRANGED IN THE SEQUENCE FOUND ON THE BALANCE SHEET AND INCOME STATEMENT, RESPECTIVELY.

HOW TRANSACTIONS ARE RECORDED

> ACCOUNTS ARE FREQUENTLY IN THE SHAPE OF A T

> THE LEFT-HAND SIDE OF THE T IS CALLED THE **DEBIT** SIDE.

> THE RIGHT-HAND SIDE OF THE T IS CALLED THE **CREDIT** SIDE.

> AN INCREASE IN AN ASSET OR AN EXPENSE ACCOUNT IS RECORDED AS A DEBIT; A DECREASE IN EITHER AN ASSET OR AN EXPENSE ACCOUNT IS RECORDED AS A CREDIT.

> AN INCREASE IN A LIABILITY, OWNERS' EQUITY OR REVENUE ACCOUNT IS RECORDED AS A CREDIT; A DECREASE IN EITHER A LIABILITY, OWNERS' EQUITY, OR REVENUE ACCOUNT IS RECORDED AS A DEBIT.

BOOKKEEPING PROCEDURES

> A TRANSACTION IS INITIALLY RECORDED IN A JOURNAL ENTRY.

> THE JOURNAL ENTRY IS THEN **POSTED** TO THE LEDGER ACCOUNTS THAT HAVE BEEN AFFECTED BY THE TRANSACTION.

KEY IDEAS

> A TRANSACTION WILL AFFECT AT LEAST TWO ACCOUNTS, AND CAN AFFECT MANY ACCOUNTS.

> BECAUSE THE BALANCE SHEET MUST BALANCE AFTER EVERY TRANSACTION, THE DEBIT(S) AND CREDIT(S) AMOUNTS OF EACH JOURNAL ENTRY MUST BE EQUAL. **DEBITS = CREDITS.**

KEY OBSERVATION

> EACH ACCOUNT HAS A "NORMAL BALANCE" SIDE - DEBIT OR CREDIT - THAT IS CONSISTENT WITH THE KIND OF ENTRY THAT CAUSES THE ACCOUNT BALANCE TO INCREASE.

> THUS, ASSET AND EXPENSE ACCOUNTS NORMALLY HAVE A DEBIT BALANCE. LIABILITY, OWNERS' EQUITY, AND REVENUE ACCOUNTS NORMALLY HAVE A CREDIT BALANCE.

AN ALTERNATIVE TO DEBIT AND CREDIT BOOKKEEPING

THE FINANCIAL STATEMENT RELATIONSHIP MODEL

BALANCE SHEET		INCOME STATEMENT
ASSETS = LIABILITIES + OWNERS' EQUITY	<---	NET INCOME = REVENUES - EXPENSES

KEY POINTS

> SHOW THE EFFECT OF EACH TRANSACTION IN THE APPROPRIATE COLUMN OF THE MODEL. SHOW ACCOUNT NAMES FOR ADDITIONAL PRECISION.

> BECAUSE NET INCOME INCREASES OWNERS' EQUITY, INCREASES IN REVENUES APPEAR AS POSITIVE AMOUNTS, AND INCREASES IN EXPENSES (WHICH DECREASE NET INCOME) APPEAR AS NEGATIVE AMOUNTS.

> KEEP THE EQUATION IN BALANCE FOR EACH TRANSACTION BY ENTERING (OR VISUALIZING) AN EQUAL SIGN BETWEEN ASSETS AND LIABILITIES.

KEY IDEA

> USE OF THIS MODEL FOCUSES ON THE IMPACT OF TRANSACTIONS ON THE FINANCIAL STATEMENTS WITHOUT CONCERN FOR BOOKKEEPING JARGON.

TRANSACTION ANALYSIS METHODOLOGY

FIVE QUESTIONS OF TRANSACTION ANALYSIS

KEY IDEA

> TO UNDERSTAND EITHER THE BOOKKEEPING PROCEDURE FOR A TRANSACTION, OR THE EFFECT OF A TRANSACTION ON THE FINANCIAL STATEMENTS, THE FOLLOWING QUESTIONS MUST BE ANSWERED.

1. **WHAT'S GOING ON?**
   (WHAT IS THE NATURE OF THE TRANSACTION?)

2. **WHAT ACCOUNTS ARE AFFECTED?**
   (WHAT IS THE FINANCIAL STATEMENT CATEGORY OF EACH ACCOUNT - ASSET, LIABILITY, OWNERS' EQUITY, REVENUE OR EXPENSE?)

3. **HOW IS EACH ACCOUNT AFFECTED?**
   (IS THE BALANCE INCREASING OR DECREASING?)

4. **DOES THE BALANCE SHEET BALANCE?**
   (DO THE DEBITS EQUAL THE CREDITS? IS THE EQUATION STILL IN BALANCE AFTER RECORDING THE TRANSACTION?)

5. **DOES MY ANALYSIS MAKE SENSE?**
   (DO THE ACCOUNT BALANCES OR THE FINANCIAL STATEMENTS REFLECT THE EFFECT OF THE TRANSACTION?)

ADJUSTING ENTRIES

WHAT ARE THEY? WHY DO THEM?

> ADJUSTING ENTRIES, OR ADJUSTMENTS, ARE "CORRECTIONS" MADE TO INCREASE THE ACCURACY OF THE INFORMATION IN THE FINANCIAL STATEMENTS.

> RECLASSIFICATIONS:
THE BOOKKEEPING FOR THE ORIGINAL TRANSACTION WAS APPROPRIATE WHEN IT WAS RECORDED, BUT THE PASSAGE OF TIME REQUIRES A RECLASSIFICATION OF THE ORIGINAL BOOKKEEPING TO REFLECT CORRECT ACCOUNT BALANCES AS OF THE DATE OF THE FINANCIAL STATEMENTS.

> ACCRUALS:
REVENUES WERE EARNED OR EXPENSES WERE INCURRED DURING THE PERIOD, BUT NO TRANSACTION WAS RECORDED, (BECAUSE NO CASH WAS RECEIVED OR PAID). IT IS NECESSARY TO **ACCRUE** THE EFFECT OF THE TRANSACTION AS OF THE DATE OF THE FINANCIAL STATEMENTS.

KEY IDEAS

> ACCRUAL ACCOUNTING MEANS THAT REVENUES ARE RECOGNIZED WHEN EARNED (NOT WHEN CASH IS RECEIVED) AND THAT EXPENSES ARE REFLECTED IN THE PERIOD IN WHICH THEY ARE INCURRED (NOT WHEN CASH IS PAID).

> ADJUSTING ENTRIES RESULT IN MATCHING REVENUES AND EXPENSES, WHICH IS THE OBJECTIVE OF ACCRUAL ACCOUNTING.

CURRENT ASSETS

DEFINITION

- CURRENT ASSETS ARE CASH AND THOSE ASSETS EXPECTED TO BE CONVERTED TO CASH OR USED UP IN THE OPERATING ACTIVITIES OF THE ENTITY WITHIN ONE YEAR.

ACCOUNTS THAT COMPRISE CURRENT ASSETS

- CASH
- MARKETABLE (OR SHORT-TERM) SECURITIES
- ACCOUNTS AND NOTES RECEIVABLE
- INVENTORIES
- PREPAID EXPENSES

KEY IDEA

- EVERY ENTITY HAS AN OPERATING CYCLE IN WHICH PRODUCTS AND SERVICES ARE PURCHASED, SERVICES ARE PERFORMED ON ACCOUNT (USUALLY), PAYMENT IS MADE TO EMPLOYEES AND SUPPLIERS, AND FINALLY CASH IS RECEIVED FROM CUSTOMERS. IF THE ENTITY IS A MANUFACTURER, PRODUCT IS MADE AND HELD AS INVENTORY BEFORE IT IS SOLD. CURRENT ASSETS REFLECT THE INVESTMENT REQUIRED TO SUPPORT THIS CYCLE.

CASH AND MARKETABLE SECURITIES

KEY IDEAS

> THE CASH AMOUNT ON THE BALANCE SHEET IS THE AMOUNT OF CASH OWNED BY THE ENTITY ON THE BALANCE SHEET DATE.

THUS THE LEDGER ACCOUNT BALANCE OF CASH MUST BE RECONCILED WITH THE BANK STATEMENT ENDING BALANCE, AND THE LEDGER ACCOUNT BALANCE MUST BE ADJUSTED AS NECESSARY.

THE ADJUSTMENT WILL REFLECT BANK TIMING DIFFERENCES AND BOOK ERRORS.

> SHORT-TERM MARKETABLE SECURITIES THAT WILL BE HELD UNTIL MATURITY ARE SHOWN ON THE BALANCE SHEET AT COST, WHICH IS USUALLY ABOUT THE SAME AS MARKET VALUE.

> SECURITIES EXPECTED TO BE HELD FOR SEVERAL MONTHS AFTER THE BALANCE SHEET DATE ARE SHOWN AT THEIR MARKET VALUE.

> INTEREST INCOME FROM MARKETABLE SECURITIES THAT HAS NOT BEEN RECEIVED MUST BE ACCRUED.

ACCOUNTS RECEIVABLE

KEY ISSUES

> ACCOUNTS RECEIVABLE ARE REPORTED ON THE BALANCE SHEET AT THEIR "NET REALIZABLE VALUE," WHICH IS THE AMOUNT OF CASH EXPECTED TO BE COLLECTED FROM THE ACCOUNTS RECEIVABLE .

> WHEN SALES ARE MADE ON ACCOUNT, THERE IS A VERY HIGH PROBABILITY THAT SOME ACCOUNTS RECEIVABLE WILL NOT BE COLLECTED.

> THE MATCHING OF REVENUES AND EXPENSES CONCEPT REQUIRES THAT THE "COST" OF UNCOLLECTIBLE ACCOUNTS RECEIVABLE BE REPORTED IN THE SAME PERIOD AS THE REVENUE THAT WAS RECOGNIZED WHEN THE ACCOUNT RECEIVABLE WAS CREATED.

KEY POINTS

> THE "COST" OF UNCOLLECTIBLE ACCOUNTS (BAD DEBTS EXPENSE) MUST BE ESTIMATED. THIS LEADS TO A VALUATION ADJUSTMENT.

> THE AMOUNT OF ACCOUNTS RECEIVABLE NOT EXPECTED TO BE COLLECTED IS RECORDED AND REPORTED IN AN "ALLOWANCE FOR BAD DEBTS" ACCOUNT.

> THE ALLOWANCE FOR BAD DEBTS ACCOUNT IS A "CONTRA ASSET" REPORTED IN THE BALANCE SHEET AS A SUBTRACTION FROM ACCOUNTS RECEIVABLE.

INTERNAL CONTROL STRUCTURE

KEY IDEA

> THE ENTITY NEEDS TO HAVE ADMINISTRATIVE CONTROLS AND ACCOUNTING CONTROLS TO SUPPORT ACHIEVEMENT OF ORGANIZATIONAL GOALS AND SOUND ACCOUNTING AND FINANCIAL REPORTING PROCEDURES.

ACCOUNTING CONTROLS

> ASSURE ACCURACY OF BOOKKEEPING RECORDS AND FINANCIAL STATEMENTS.

> PROTECT ASSETS FROM UNAUTHORIZED USE OR LOSS.

ADMINISTRATIVE CONTROLS

> ENCOURAGE ADHERENCE TO MANAGEMENT'S POLICIES.

> PROVIDE FOR EFFICIENT OPERATIONS.

KEY OBSERVATION

> INTERNAL CONTROLS ARE POSITIVE; THEY SUPPORT ACHIEVEMENT OF ORGANIZATIONAL OBJECTIVES.

INVENTORIES

WHAT'S GOING ON?

> THE INVENTORY ASSET ACCOUNT CONTAINS THE COST OF ITEMS THAT ARE BEING HELD FOR SALE. WHEN AN ITEM OF INVENTORY IS SOLD, ITS COST IS TRANSFERRED FROM THE INVENTORY ASSET ACCOUNT (IN THE BALANCE SHEET) TO THE COST OF GOODS SOLD EXPENSE ACCOUNT (IN THE INCOME STATEMENT).

THIS IS A TRANSACTION SEPARATE FROM THE SALE TRANSACTION, WHICH RESULTS IN AN INCREASE IN AN ASSET ACCOUNT IN THE BALANCE SHEET (EITHER ACCOUNTS RECEIVABLE OR CASH), AND AN INCREASE IN SALES, A REVENUE ACCOUNT IN THE INCOME STATEMENT.

KEY ISSUE

> WHEN THE INVENTORY INCLUDES THE COST OF SEVERAL UNITS OF THE ITEM SOLD, HOW IS THE COST OF THE ITEM SOLD DETERMINED?

INVENTORY COST FLOW ASSUMPTIONS

ALTERNATIVE COST FLOW ASSUMPTIONS

> SPECIFIC IDENTIFICATION

> WEIGHTED AVERAGE

> FIFO - FIRST COST IN TO INVENTORY,
FIRST COST OUT TO COST OF GOODS SOLD

> LIFO - LAST COST IN TO INVENTORY,
FIRST COST OUT TO COST OF GOODS SOLD

KEY ISSUES

> HOW DO CHANGES IN THE COST OF INVENTORY ITEMS OVER TIME AFFECT COST OF GOODS SOLD EX UNDER EACH OF THE COST FLOW ASSUMPTIONS?

> HOW DO CHANGES IN THE QUANTITY OF INVENTORY ITEMS AFFECT COST OF GOODS SOLD UNDER EACH OF THE COST FLOW ASSUMPTIONS?

KEY POINT

> ROI, ROE, AND MEASURES OF LIQUIDITY WILL BE AFFECTED BY THE INVENTORY COST FLOW ASSUMPTION USED WHEN THE COST OF INVENTORY ITEMS CHANGES OVER TIME.

PREPAID EXPENSES

WHAT'S GOING ON?

> PREPAID EXPENSES RESULT FROM THE APPLICATION OF ACCRUAL ACCOUNTING. SOME EXPENDITURES MADE IN ONE PERIOD ARE NOT PROPERLY RECOGNIZABLE AS EXPENSES UNTIL A SUBSEQUENT PERIOD.

IN THESE SITUATIONS, EXPENSE RECOGNITION IS **DEFERRED** UNTIL THE PERIOD IN WHICH THE EXPENSE APPLIES.

PREPAID EXPENSES FREQUENTLY INCLUDE:

> INSURANCE PREMIUMS

> RENT

LONG-LIVED ASSETS

KEY TERMINOLOGY

> DEPRECIATION EXPENSE / ACCUMULATED DEPRECIATION

DEPRECIATION EXPENSE REFERS TO THAT PORTION OF THE COST OF A LONG-LIVED ASSET RECORDED AS AN EXPENSE IN AN ACCOUNTING PERIOD. DEPRECIATION IN ACCOUNTING IS THE SPREADING OF THE COST OF A LONG-LIVED ASSET OVER ITS ESTIMATED USEFUL LIFE TO THE ENTITY. THIS IS AN APPLICATION OF THE MATCHING CONCEPT.

ACCUMULATED DEPRECIATION IS A CONTRA ASSET ACCOUNT. THE BALANCE IN THIS ACCOUNT IS THE ACCUMULATED TOTAL OF ALL OF THE DEPRECIATION EXPENSE RECOGNIZED TO DATE ON THE RELATED ASSET(S).

> CAPITALIZE / EXPENSE

TO **CAPITALIZE** AN EXPENDITURE MEANS TO RECORD THE EXPENDITURE AS AN ASSET. A LONG-LIVED ASSET THAT HAS BEEN CAPITALIZED WILL BE DEPRECIATED.

TO **EXPENSE** AN EXPENDITURE MEANS TO RECORD THE EXPENDITURE AS AN EXPENSE.

> NET BOOK VALUE

THE DIFFERENCE BETWEEN AN ASSET'S COST AND ITS ACCUMULATED DEPRECIATION IS ITS **NET BOOK VALUE**.

DEPRECIATION OF LONG-LIVED ASSETS

KEY POINT

> THE RECOGNITION OF DEPRECIATION EXPENSE DOES NOT AFFECT CASH.

DEPRECIATION EXPENSE CALCULATION ELEMENTS

> ASSET COST

> ESTIMATED SALVAGE VALUE

> ESTIMATED USEFUL LIFE TO ENTITY

ALTERNATIVE CALCULATION METHODS

> STRAIGHT-LINE

- BASED ON YEARS OF LIFE
- BASED ON UNITS OF PRODUCTION

> ACCELERATED

- SUM-OF-THE-YEARS-DIGITS
- DECLINING-BALANCE

DEPRECIATION METHOD ALTERNATIVES

KEY POINTS

> ACCELERATED DEPRECIATION RESULTS IN GREATER DEPRECIATION EXPENSE DURING THE EARLY YEARS OF THE ASSET'S LIFE THAN STRAIGHT-LINE DEPRECIATION. MOST FIRMS USE STRAIGHT-LINE DEPRECIATION FOR FINANCIAL REPORTING PURPOSES.

> DEPRECIATION EXPENSE DOES NOT AFFECT CASH. BUT BECAUSE DEPRECIATION IS DEDUCTIBLE FOR INCOME TAX PURPOSES, MOST FIRMS USE AN ACCELERATED METHOD FOR CALCULATING INCOME TAX DEPRECIATION.

> THE DEPRECIATION METHOD SELECTED FOR FINANCIAL REPORTING PURPOSES WILL HAVE AN EFFECT ON ROI AND ROE. TO MAKE VALID COMPARISONS BETWEEN COMPANIES, IT IS NECESSARY TO KNOW WHETHER OR NOT COMPARABLE DEPRECIATION CALCULATION METHODS HAVE BEEN USED.

> IF AN EXPENDITURE HAS BEEN INAPPROPRIATELY CAPITALIZED OR EXPENSED, BOTH ASSETS AND NET INCOME WILL BE AFFECTED, IN THE CURRENT YEAR AND IN FUTURE YEARS OF THE ASSET'S LIFE.

PRESENT VALUE ANALYSIS

KEY IDEAS

> MONEY HAS VALUE OVER TIME.

> AN AMOUNT TO BE RECEIVED OR PAID IN THE FUTURE HAS A VALUE TODAY (PRESENT VALUE) THAT IS LESS THAN THE FUTURE VALUE.

WHY? BECAUSE OF THE INTEREST THAT CAN BE EARNED BETWEEN THE PRESENT AND THE FUTURE.

KEY RELATIONSHIP

> A TIME LINE APPROACH CREATES A VISUAL IMAGE THAT MAKES THE TIME VALUE OF MONEY CONCEPT EASY TO WORK WITH.

WHAT IS THE PRESENT VALUE OF $ 4,000 TO BE RECEIVED OR PAID IN 4 YEARS, AT AN INTEREST RATE OF 8%?

```
                INTEREST RATE = 8%
TODAY        1          2          3          4
--------------------------------------------------------------
     AMOUNT DUE IN 4 YEARS                          $ 4,000
   PRESENT VALUE FACTOR (TABLE 6-2)               * .7350
                                                  ---------
$ 2,940 <-----------------------------------------------┘
```

THE VALUE TODAY OF $ 4,000 TO BE PAID OR RECEIVED IN 4 YEARS, ASSUMING AN INTEREST RATE OF 8%, IS $ 2,940.

ASSETS ACQUIRED BY CAPITAL LEASE

KEY IDEAS

> A LONG-TERM LEASE IS FREQUENTLY A WAY OF FINANCING THE ACQUISITION OF A LONG-LIVED ASSET.

> THE EFFECT OF THE ACCOUNTING FOR A LEASED ASSET SHOULD NOT BE DIFFERENT FROM THE ACCOUNTING FOR A PURCHASED ASSET.

ACCOUNTING FOR A LEASED ASSET

> THE "COST" OF A LEASED ASSET IS THE PRESENT VALUE OF THE LEASE OBLIGATIONS.

> DEPRECIATION EXPENSE IS RECORDED BASED ON THIS "COST".

> AS ANNUAL LEASE PAYMENTS ARE MADE, INTEREST EXPENSE IS RECOGNIZED AND THE LEASE OBLIGATION IS REDUCED.

INTANGIBLE ASSETS AND NATURAL RESOURCES

KEY POINT

> ALTHOUGH THE TERMINOLOGY IS DIFFERENT FROM THAT USED FOR DEPRECIABLE ASSETS, THE ACCOUNTING IS ESSENTIALLY THE SAME: THE EXPENDITURE IS CAPITALIZED, AND THE EXPENSE IS RECOGNIZED PERIODICALLY OVER THE USEFUL LIFE OF THE ASSET TO THE ENTITY.

TERMINOLOGY

> **INTANGIBLE ASSETS**

AMORTIZATION EXPENSE

USUALLY AN ACCUMULATED AMORTIZATION ACCOUNT IS NOT USED.

> **NATURAL RESOURCES**

DEPLETION EXPENSE

ACCUMULATED DEPLETION

CURRENT LIABILITIES

DEFINITION

> CURRENT LIABILITIES ARE THOSE THAT MUST BE PAID WITHIN ONE YEAR OF THE BALANCE SHEET DATE.

ACCOUNTS THAT COMPRISE CURRENT LIABILITIES

> SHORT-TERM DEBT

> ACCOUNTS PAYABLE

> VARIOUS ACCRUED LIABILITIES

INCLUDES WAGES, OPERATING EXPENSES, INTEREST, TAXES

> CURRENT MATURITIES OF LONG-TERM DEBT

KEY IDEAS

> A PRINCIPAL CONCERN ABOUT LIABILITIES IS THAT THEY ARE NOT UNDERSTATED. IF LIABILITIES ARE TOO LOW, EXPENSES ARE PROBABLY UNDERSTATED ALSO, WHICH MEANS THAT NET INCOME IS OVERSTATED.

> THE AMOUNT OF CURRENT LIABILITIES IS RELATED TO THE AMOUNT OF CURRENT ASSETS TO MEASURE THE FIRM'S **LIQUIDITY**, ITS ABILITY TO PAY ITS BILLS WHEN THEY COME DUE.

INTEREST CALCULATION METHODS

BASIC MODEL FOR CALCULATING INTEREST

INTEREST = **PRINCIPAL** X ANNUAL **RATE** X **TIME** IN YEARS

KEY ISSUE

> IS THE PRINCIPAL AMOUNT USED IN THE INTEREST CALCULATION EQUAL TO THE CASH ACTUALLY AVAILABLE FOR THE BORROWER TO USE?

STRAIGHT INTEREST

> PRINCIPAL USED IN THE INTEREST CALCULATION IS EQUAL TO THE CASH RECEIVED BY THE BORROWER.

> INTEREST IS PAID TO THE LENDER PERIODICALLY DURING THE TERM OF THE LOAN, OR AT THE LOAN MATURITY DATE.

DISCOUNT

> PRINCIPAL USED IN THE INTEREST CALCULATION IS THE "AMOUNT BORROWED", BUT THEN INTEREST IS SUBTRACTED FROM THAT PRINCIPAL TO GET THE AMOUNT OF CASH MADE AVAILABLE TO THE BORROWER. THIS RESULTS IN AN EFFECTIVE INTEREST RATE (APR) GREATER THAN THE RATE USED IN THE INTEREST CALCULATION.

> BECAUSE INTEREST WAS PAID IN ADVANCE, ONLY THE PRINCIPAL AMOUNT IS REPAID AT THE LOAN MATURITY DATE.

FINANCIAL LEVERAGE

KEY IDEAS

> WHEN MONEY IS BORROWED AT A FIXED INTEREST RATE, THE DIFFERENCE BETWEEN THE ROI EARNED ON THAT MONEY AND THE INTEREST RATE PAID AFFECTS THE WEALTH OF THE BORROWER. THIS IS CALLED FINANCIAL LEVERAGE.

> FINANCIAL LEVERAGE IS POSITIVE WHEN THE ROI EARNED ON BORROWED MONEY IS GREATER THAN THE INTEREST RATE PAID ON THE BORROWED MONEY. FINANCIAL LEVERAGE IS NEGATIVE WHEN THE OPPOSITE OCCURS.

> FINANCIAL LEVERAGE INCREASES THE RISK THAT A FIRM'S ROI WILL FLUCTUATE, BECAUSE ROI CHANGES AS BUSINESS CONDITIONS AND THE FIRM'S OPERATING RESULTS CHANGE, BUT THE INTEREST RATE ON BORROWED FUNDS IS USUALLY FIXED.

LONG-TERM DEBT (BONDS PAYABLE)

KEY IDEA

> FIRMS ISSUE LONG-TERM DEBT (BONDS PAYABLE) TO GET SOME OF THE FUNDS NEEDED TO INVEST IN ASSETS. THE OWNERS DO NOT USUALLY PROVIDE ALL OF THE NECESSARY FUNDS BECAUSE IT IS USUALLY DESIRABLE TO HAVE SOME FINANCIAL LEVERAGE.

BOND CHARACTERISTICS

> A FIXED INTEREST RATE (USUALLY). CALLED THE **STATED** RATE OR **COUPON** RATE.

> INTEREST USUALLY PAYABLE QUARTERLY OR SEMI-ANNUALLY.

> INDIVIDUAL BONDS USUALLY HAVE A FACE AMOUNT (PRINCIPAL) OF $ 1,000.

> BOND PRICES ARE STATED AS A % OF THE FACE AMOUNT; FOR EXAMPLE, A PRICE QUOTE OF 98.3 MEANS 98.3% OF $ 1000, OR $ 983.

> MOST BONDS HAVE A STATED MATURITY DATE - BUT MOST BONDS ARE ALSO **CALLABLE**; THEY CAN BE REDEEMED PRIOR TO MATURITY AT THE OPTION OF THE ISSUER.

> FREQUENTLY SOME COLLATERAL IS PROVIDED BY THE ISSUER.

BOND MARKET VALUE

KEY POINT

> THE MARKET VALUE OF A BOND IS A FUNCTION OF THE RELATIONSHIP BETWEEN MARKET INTEREST RATES AND THE BOND'S STATED OR COUPON RATE OF INTEREST.
>
> AS MARKET INTEREST RATES FALL, THE MARKET VALUE OF A BOND RISES.
>
> AS MARKET INTEREST RATES RISE, THE MARKET VALUE OF A BOND FALLS.

WHAT'S GOING ON?

> A BOND'S STATED OR COUPON RATE OF INTEREST IS FIXED AND STAYS THE SAME REGARDLESS OF WHAT HAPPENS TO MARKET INTEREST RATES. THEREFORE, IF MARKET INTEREST RATES RISE ABOVE THE STATED OR COUPON RATE, THE BOND BECOMES LESS VALUABLE TO INVESTORS.

KEY RELATIONSHIP

> THE MARKET VALUE OF A BOND IS THE PRESENT VALUE OF THE FUTURE PAYMENTS OF INTEREST AND PRINCIPAL, BASED ON (DISCOUNTED AT) MARKET INTEREST RATES.

BOND PREMIUM AND DISCOUNT

KEY IDEA

> WHEN THE MARKET INTEREST RATE AT THE DATE A BOND IS ISSUED IS DIFFERENT FROM THE STATED OR COUPON RATE OF THE BOND, THE BOND WILL BE ISSUED AT:

> A PREMIUM (MARKET INTEREST RATE < STATED OR COUPON RATE)

> OR A DISCOUNT (MARKET INTEREST RATE > STATED OR COUPON RATE).

KEY POINTS

> WHEN A BOND IS ISSUED AT A PREMIUM, THE PREMIUM IS AMORTIZED TO INTEREST EXPENSE OVER THE TERM OF THE BOND, RESULTING IN LOWER ANNUAL INTEREST EXPENSE THAN THE INTEREST PAID ON THE BOND.

> WHEN A BOND IS ISSUED AT A DISCOUNT, THE DISCOUNT IS AMORTIZED TO INTEREST EXPENSE OVER THE TERM OF THE BOND, RESULTING IN HIGHER ANNUAL INTEREST EXPENSE THAN THE INTEREST PAID ON THE BOND.

> THE AMORTIZATION OF PREMIUM OR DISCOUNT RESULTS IN REPORTING AN ACTUAL INTEREST EXPENSE FROM THE BONDS THAT IS A FUNCTION OF THE MARKET INTEREST RATE WHEN THE BONDS WERE ISSUED - AN APPROPRIATE RESULT.

DEFERRED INCOME TAXES

WHAT'S GOING ON?

> DIFFERENCES BETWEEN BOOK AND TAXABLE INCOME ARISE BECAUSE FINANCIAL ACCOUNTING METHODS DIFFER FROM ACCOUNTING METHODS PERMITTED FOR INCOME TAX PURPOSES.

EXAMPLE: BOOK DEPRECIATION IS USUALLY CALCULATED ON A STRAIGHT-LINE BASIS, AND TAX DEPRECIATION IS USUALLY BASED ON AN ACCELERATED METHOD.

KEY ISSUE

> WHEN TAXABLE INCOME IS DIFFERENT FROM BOOK INCOME, INCOME TAX EXPENSE SHOULD BE A FUNCTION OF BOOK INCOME BEFORE TAXES, NOT TAXABLE INCOME. THIS IS AN APPLICATION OF THE MATCHING CONCEPT.

KEY IDEA

> INCOME TAX EXPENSE BASED ON BOOK INCOME IS USUALLY MORE THAN THE INCOME TAXES CURRENTLY PAYABLE. THE DIFFERENCE IS SHOWN AS A LIABILITY CALLED "DEFERRED FEDERAL INCOME TAXES". THIS LIABILITY WILL BECOME CURRENT WHEN TAXABLE INCOME EXCEEDS BOOK INCOME.

EXAMPLE: LATE IN AN ASSET'S LIFE, THE AMOUNT OF TAX DEPRECIATION IS LESS THAN THE AMOUNT OF BOOK DEPRECIATION.

OWNERS' EQUITY - PAID-IN CAPITAL

ACCOUNTS INCLUDED IN PAID-IN CAPITAL

> COMMON STOCK (SOMETIMES CALLED CAPITAL STOCK)

> PREFERRED STOCK (IF AUTHORIZED BY THE CORPORATION'S CHARTER)

> ADDITIONAL PAID-IN CAPITAL

KEY TERMINOLOGY FOR NUMBER OF SHARES OF STOCK

> AUTHORIZED - BY THE CORPORATION'S CHARTER

> ISSUED - SOLD IN THE PAST TO STOCKHOLDERS

> OUTSTANDING - STILL HELD BY STOCKHOLDERS

> TREASURY STOCK - SHARES OF ITS OWN STOCK PURCHASED AND HELD BY THE CORPORATION. THE NUMBER OF SHARES OF TREASURY STOCK IS THE DIFFERENCE BETWEEN THE NUMBER OF SHARES ISSUED AND THE NUMBER OF SHARES OUTSTANDING.

KEY TERMINOLOGY FOR STOCK VALUE

> PAR VALUE - AN ARBITRARY AMOUNT ASSIGNED TO EACH SHARE AT INCORPORATION. THE FIRM CAN ISSUE NO-PAR VALUE STOCK. IF NO-PAR VALUE STOCK HAS A "STATED VALUE", THE STATED VALUE IS LIKE A PAR VALUE.

COMMON STOCK AND PREFERRED STOCK

KEY IDEAS

> COMMON STOCK REPRESENTS THE BASIC OWNERSHIP OF A CORPORATION.

> PREFERRED STOCK REPRESENTS OWNERSHIP, BUT HAS SOME PREFERENCES RELATIVE TO COMMON STOCK. THESE INCLUDE:

PRIORITY CLAIM TO DIVIDENDS, AND

PRIORITY CLAIM TO ASSETS IN LIQUIDATION.

HOWEVER, PREFERRED STOCKHOLDERS ARE NOT USUALLY ENTITLED TO VOTE FOR DIRECTORS.

KEY POINTS ABOUT DIVIDENDS ON PREFERRED STOCK

> DIVIDENDS ARE USUALLY "CUMULATIVE," WHICH MEANS THAT DIVIDENDS NOT PAID DURING ONE YEAR (IN ARREARS) MUST BE PAID IN A FUTURE YEAR BEFORE DIVIDENDS CAN BE PAID ON COMMON STOCK.

> DIVIDEND AMOUNT IS EXPRESSED AS A CERTAIN AMOUNT PER SHARE ($3.50), OR AS A PERCENT OF PAR VALUE (7% OF PAR VALUE OF $ 50).

PAID-IN CAPITAL AMOUNTS ON THE BALANCE SHEET

WHAT'S GOING ON?

> IF THE STOCK HAS A PAR VALUE, THE AMOUNTS OPPOSITE THE STOCK CAPTIONS ARE ALWAYS PAR VALUE MULTIPLIED BY THE NUMBER OF SHARES ISSUED.

THE DIFFERENCE BETWEEN THE PAR VALUE AND THE AMOUNT RECEIVED PER SHARE WHEN THE STOCK WAS ISSUED IS RECORDED AS ADDITIONAL PAID-IN CAPITAL.

> IF THE STOCK IS NO-PAR VALUE STOCK (WITHOUT A STATED VALUE), THE AMOUNT OPPOSITE THE CAPTION IS THE TOTAL AMOUNT RECEIVED WHEN THE STOCK WAS ISSUED.

RETAINED EARNINGS AND DIVIDENDS

KEY IDEAS

> RETAINED EARNINGS INCREASES EACH PERIOD BY THE AMOUNT OF NET INCOME FOR THAT PERIOD. (NET LOSSES DECREASE RETAINED EARNINGS.)

> DIVIDENDS ARE DISTRIBUTIONS OF RETAINED EARNINGS TO THE STOCKHOLDERS, AND ARE A REDUCTION IN RETAINED EARNINGS.

> CASH DIVIDENDS ARE DECLARED BY THE BOARD OF DIRECTORS AS AN AMOUNT PER SHARE.

> STOCK DIVIDENDS ARE DECLARED BY THE BOARD OF DIRECTORS AS A PERCENTAGE OF CURRENTLY ISSUED SHARES. STOCK DIVIDENDS AFFECT ONLY RETAINED EARNINGS AND PAID-IN CAPITAL; ASSETS AND LIABILITIES ARE NOT AFFECTED.

> CASH DIVIDENDS ARE NOT PAID ON TREASURY STOCK. STOCK DIVIDENDS ARE USUALLY ISSUED ON TREASURY STOCK.

STOCK SPLITS

KEY IDEA

> A STOCK SPLIT INVOLVES ISSUING ADDITIONAL SHARES OF STOCK IN PROPORTION TO THE NUMBER OF SHARES CURRENTLY OWNED BY EACH STOCKHOLDER. THE RELATIVE OWNERSHIP INTEREST OF EACH STOCKHOLDER DOES NOT CHANGE.

> BECAUSE THERE ARE MORE SHARES OF STOCK OUTSTANDING, THE MARKET PRICE OF EACH SHARE WILL FALL TO REFLECT THE SPLIT.

BALANCE SHEET EFFECT OF STOCK SPLIT

> DOLLAR AMOUNTS ON THE BALANCE SHEET ARE NOT AFFECTED. THE PAR VALUE IS REDUCED, AND THE NUMBER OF SHARES ISSUED IS INCREASED.

INCOME STATEMENT

MULTIPLE-STEP MODEL

CRUISERS, INC., AND SUBSIDIARIES
Consolidated Income Statement
For the Years Ended August 31, 1996, and 1995
(000 omitted)

	1996	*1995*
Net sales	$77,543	$62,531
Cost of goods sold	48,077	39,870
Gross profit	$29,466	$22,661
Selling, general, and administrative expenses	23,264	18,425
Income from operations	$ 6,202	$ 4,236
Other income (expense):		
Interest expense	(3,378)	(2,679)
Other income (net)	385	193
Minority interest	(432)	(356)
Income before taxes	$ 2,777	$ 1,394
Provision for income taxes	1,250	630
Net income	$ 1,527	$ 764
Earnings per share of common stock outstanding	$ 5.56	$ 2.42

KEY OBSERVATIONS

> THERE IS A GREAT DEAL OF SUMMARIZATION.

> CAPTIONS REFLECT THE REVENUE AND EXPENSE CATEGORIES THAT ARE MOST SIGNIFICANT TO UNDERSTANDING RESULTS OF OPERATIONS.

> INCOME FROM OPERATIONS IS SOMETIMES MORE MEANINGFUL FOR TREND COMPARISONS THAN NET INCOME.

LINKAGE BETWEEN BALANCE SHEET AND INCOME STATEMENT ACCOUNTS

BALANCE SHEET		**INCOME STATEMENT**
ACCOUNTS RECEIVABLE	-------->	SALES / REVENUES
NOTES RECEIVABLE AND SHORT-TERM INVESTMENTS	------->	INTEREST INCOME
INVENTORIES	------------------------>	COST OF GOODS SOLD
PREPAID EXPENSES AND ACCRUED LIABILITIES	------->	OPERATING EXPENSES
ACCUMULATED DEPRECIATION	--------------------->	DEPRECIATION EXPENSE (REPORTED IN COST OF GOODS SOLD AND OPERATING EXP.)
NOTES PAYABLE AND BONDS PAYABLE	------------>	INTEREST EXPENSE
INCOME TAXES PAYABLE AND DEFERRED TAX LIABILITY	------->	INCOME TAX EXPENSE

STATEMENT OF CASH FLOWS

WHAT'S GOING ON?

> THE INCOME STATEMENT REPORTS ACCRUAL BASIS NET INCOME. FINANCIAL STATEMENT USERS ALSO WANT TO KNOW ABOUT THE FIRM'S CASH FLOWS.

> THE REASONS FOR THE CHANGE IN CASH FROM THE BEGINNING TO THE END OF THE PERIOD ARE SUMMARIZED IN THREE CATEGORIES:

> CASH FLOWS FROM **OPERATING** ACTIVITIES

> CASH FLOWS FROM **INVESTING** ACTIVITIES

> CASH FLOWS FROM **FINANCING** ACTIVITIES

INTERPRETING THE STATEMENT OF CASH FLOWS

KEY QUESTIONS

> WHAT HAPPENED TO THE CASH BALANCE DURING THE YEAR?

> WHAT IS THE RELATIONSHIP BETWEEN CASH FLOWS FROM OPERATING, INVESTING, AND FINANCING ACTIVITIES?

KEY RELATIONSHIPS TO OBSERVE

> DID CASH FLOWS FROM OPERATING ACTIVITIES EXCEED CASH USED FOR INVESTING ACTIVITIES?

> DID FINANCING ACTIVITIES CAUSE A NET INCREASE OR NET DECREASE IN CASH?

> IN OPERATING ACTIVITIES, WHAT WERE THE EFFECTS OF ACCOUNTS RECEIVABLE, INVENTORY, AND ACCOUNTS PAYABLE CHANGES?

> IN INVESTING ACTIVITIES, WHAT WAS THE RELATIONSHIP BETWEEN THE INVESTMENT IN NEW ASSETS AND THE SALE OF OLD ASSETS?

> IN FINANCING ACTIVITIES, WHAT WERE THE NET EFFECTS OF LONG-TERM DEBT AND CAPITAL STOCK CHANGES? WHAT WAS THE EFFECT OF CASH DIVIDENDS PAID?

EXPLANATORY NOTES TO FINANCIAL STATEMENTS

KEY POINT

> FINANCIAL STATEMENT READERS MUST BE ABLE TO LEARN ABOUT THE FOLLOWING KEY ISSUES THAT AFFECT THEIR ABILITY TO UNDERSTAND THE STATEMENTS:

> DEPRECIATION METHODS

> INVENTORY COST FLOW ASSUMPTIONS

> CURRENT AND DEFERRED INCOME TAXES

> EMPLOYEE BENEFIT INFORMATION

> EARNINGS PER SHARE OF COMMON STOCK DETAILS

> STOCK OPTION AND STOCK PURCHASE PLAN INFORMATION

OTHER KEY DISCLOSURES

> MANAGEMENT'S STATEMENT OF RESPONSIBILITY

> MANAGEMENT'S DISCUSSION AND ANALYSIS

KEY IDEA

> THE EXPLANATORY NOTES TO THE FINANCIAL STATEMENTS MUST BE REVIEWED TO HAVE A REASONABLY COMPLETE UNDERSTANDING OF WHAT THE NUMBERS MEAN.

FIVE-YEAR (OR LONGER) SUMMARY OF FINANCIAL DATA

KEY IDEAS

> LOOK AT TREND OF DATA.

> NOTICE THE EFFECT OF STOCK DIVIDENDS AND STOCK SPLITS ON PER SHARE DATA.

> USE THE DATA REPORTED FOR PRIOR YEARS TO MAKE RATIO CALCULATIONS FOR EVALUATIVE PURPOSES.

INDEPENDENT AUDITORS' REPORT

KEY IDEA

> FINANCIAL STATEMENTS PRESENT FAIRLY, **IN ALL MATERIAL RESPECTS**, THE FINANCIAL POSITION AND RESULTS OF OPERATIONS.

KEY POINT

> AUDITORS GIVE NO GUARANTEE THAT FINANCIAL STATEMENTS ARE FREE FROM ERROR OR FRAUD.

LIQUIDITY ANALYSIS

KEY QUESTION

> IS THE FIRM LIKELY TO BE ABLE TO PAY ITS OBLIGATIONS WHEN THEY COME DUE?

LIQUIDITY MEASURES

> WORKING CAPITAL

> CURRENT RATIO

> ACID-TEST RATIO

KEY ISSUE

> THE INVENTORY COST FLOW ASSUMPTION USED BY THE FIRM (FIFO, LIFO, WEIGHTED AVERAGE. OR SPECIFIC IDENTIFICATION) WILL AFFECT THESE MEASURES.

ACTIVITY MEASURES

KEY QUESTION

> HOW EFFICIENTLY ARE THE FIRM'S ASSETS BEING USED?

ACTIVITY MEASURES

> ACCOUNTS RECEIVABLE TURNOVER (OR NUMBER OF DAY'S SALES IN ACCOUNTS RECEIVABLE)

> INVENTORY TURNOVER (OR NUMBER OF DAY'S SALES IN INVENTORY)

> PLANT AND EQUIPMENT TURNOVER

> TOTAL ASSET TURNOVER

GENERAL MODEL

$$\text{> TURNOVER} = \frac{\text{SALES FOR PERIOD}}{\text{AVERAGE ASSET BALANCE FOR PERIOD}}$$

KEY IDEAS

> INVENTORY ACTIVITY CALCULATIONS USE COST OF GOODS SOLD INSTEAD OF SALES.

> NUMBER OF DAY'S SALES CALCULATIONS USE THE ENDING BALANCE OF THE ASSET ACCOUNT DIVIDED BY AVERAGE DAILY SALES OR AVERAGE DAILY COST OF GOODS SOLD.

PROFITABILITY MEASURES

KEY QUESTIONS

> WHAT RATE OF RETURN HAS BEEN EARNED ON ASSETS OR OWNERS' EQUITY?

> HOW EXPENSIVE IS THE FIRM'S COMMON STOCK RELATIVE TO OTHER COMPANIES, AND WHAT HAS BEEN THE DIVIDEND EXPERIENCE?

PROFITABILITY MEASURES

> ROI - RETURN ON INVESTMENT

> ROE - RETURN ON EQUITY

> PRICE / EARNINGS RATIO (EARNINGS MULTIPLE)

> DIVIDEND YIELD

> DIVIDEND PAYOUT RATIO

KEY IDEAS

> FACTORS IN ROI CALCULATION MAY DIFFER AMONG COMPANIES (NET INCOME OR OPERATING INCOME IN THE NUMERATOR); WHAT IS IMPORTANT IS THE CONSISTENCY OF DEFINITION, AND **TREND** OF ROI.

> ROE IS BASED ON THE NET INCOME APPLICABLE TO, AND THE EQUITY OF, **COMMON STOCKHOLDERS**.

FINANCIAL LEVERAGE RATIOS

KEY IDEA

> FINANCIAL LEVERAGE REFERS TO THE USE OF DEBT (INSTEAD OF OWNERS' EQUITY) TO FINANCE THE ACQUISITION OF ASSETS FOR THE FIRM.

THE INTEREST RATE ON DEBT IS FIXED, SO IF THE ROI EARNED ON THE BORROWED FUNDS IS GREATER THAN THE INTEREST RATE OWED, ROE WILL INCREASE. THIS IS REFERRED TO AS "POSITIVE" FINANCIAL LEVERAGE.

IF THE ROI EARNED ON BORROWED FUNDS IS LESS THAN THE INTEREST RATE OWED, ROE WILL DECREASE. THIS IS REFERRED TO AS "NEGATIVE" FINANCIAL LEVERAGE.

KEY QUESTIONS

> HOW MUCH FINANCIAL LEVERAGE IS THE FIRM USING?

> HOW MUCH RISK OF FINANCIAL LOSS TO CREDITORS AND OWNERS IS THERE?

FINANCIAL LEVERAGE RATIOS

> DEBT RATIO

> DEBT/EQUITY RATIO

> TIMES INTEREST EARNED RATIO

OTHER ANALYTICAL TECHNIQUES

BOOK VALUE PER SHARE OF COMMON STOCK

KEY IDEA

> AN EASILY CALCULATED AMOUNT BASED ON THE BALANCE SHEET AMOUNT OF OWNERS' EQUITY. BUT NOT VERY USEFUL IN MOST CASES BECAUSE BALANCE SHEET AMOUNTS DO NOT REFLECT MARKET VALUES OR REPLACEMENT VALUES.

COMMON SIZE FINANCIAL STATEMENTS

KEY IDEA

> COMPARISONS BETWEEN FIRMS (OR BETWEEN PERIODS FOR THE SAME FIRM) CAN BE MORE EASILY UNDERSTOOD IF FINANCIAL STATEMENT AMOUNTS ARE EXPRESSED AS PERCENTAGES OF TOTAL ASSETS OR TOTAL REVENUES.

OTHER OPERATING STATISTICS

KEY IDEA

> NOT ALL DECISIONS AND INFORMED JUDGMENTS ABOUT AN ENTITY ARE BASED ON FINANCIAL DATA. NONFINANCIAL STATISTICS ARE FREQUENTLY RELEVANT AND USEFUL.

MANAGERIAL ACCOUNTING COMPARED TO FINANCIAL ACCOUNTING

KEY CHARACTERISTICS THAT DIFFER

> SERVICE PERSPECTIVE

> BREADTH OF CONCERN

> REPORTING FREQUENCY AND PROMPTNESS

> DEGREE OF PRECISION OF DATA USED

> REPORTING STANDARDS

COST CLASSIFICATIONS

KEY IDEA

> THERE ARE DIFFERENT COSTS FOR DIFFERENT PURPOSES.

COST CLASSIFICATIONS

> FOR COST ACCOUNTING PURPOSES:

PRODUCT COST
PERIOD COST

> RELATIONSHIP TO PRODUCT OR ACTIVITY:

DIRECT COST
INDIRECT COST

> RELATIONSHIP BETWEEN TOTAL COST AND VOLUME OF ACTIVITY:

VARIABLE COST
FIXED COST

> TIME-FRAME PERSPECTIVE:

CONTROLLABLE COST
NONCONTROLLABLE COST

> FOR OTHER ANALYTICAL PURPOSES:

DIFFERENTIAL COST
ALLOCATED COST
SUNK COST
OPPORTUNITY COST

COST ACCOUNTING SYSTEMS

KEY IDEAS

> PERIOD COSTS (SELLING, GENERAL, AND ADMINISTRATIVE) ARE ACCOUNTED FOR AS EXPENSES IN THE PERIOD INCURRED.

> PRODUCT COSTS FLOW THROUGH INVENTORY (ASSET) ACCOUNTS, AND THEN TO THE COST OF GOODS SOLD (EXPENSE) ACCOUNT.

RAW MATERIAL, DIRECT LABOR, AND **MANUFACTURING OVERHEAD** COSTS ARE CAPITALIZED AS INVENTORY -----> UNTIL THE PRODUCT THEY RELATE TO IS SOLD.

> RAW MATERIAL AND DIRECT LABOR COSTS ARE RATHER EASILY IDENTIFIED WITH THE PRODUCT. MANUFACTURING OVERHEAD IS "APPLIED" TO PRODUCTION BASED ON A **PREDETERMINED OVERHEAD APPLICATION RATE**, DETERMINED AS FOLLOWS:

$$\frac{\text{ESTIMATED OVERHEAD COSTS FOR THE YEAR}}{\text{ESTIMATED ACTIVITY FOR THE YEAR}}$$

KEY POINT

> BECAUSE THE PREDETERMINED OVERHEAD APPLICATION RATE IS BASED ON ESTIMATES, THERE WILL PROBABLY BE "OVERAPPLIED" OR "UNDERAPPLIED" OVERHEAD AT THE END OF THE YEAR. THIS AMOUNT USUALLY BECOMES PART OF COST OF GOODS SOLD.

COST OF GOODS MANUFACTURED AND COST OF GOODS SOLD

KEY IDEA

> BECAUSE OF THE INVENTORY ACCOUNTS, COST OF GOODS MANUFACTURED AND COST OF GOODS SOLD ARE NOT SIMPLY THE TOTALS OF COSTS INCURRED DURING THE PERIOD.

KEY MODEL

> COST OF GOODS MANUFACTURED:

RAW MATERIALS INVENTORY, BEGINNING
+ RAW MATERIALS PURCHASES
- RAW MATERIALS INVENTORY, ENDING
= COST OF RAW MATERIALS USED
+ WORK-IN-PROCESS INVENTORY, BEGINNING
+ DIRECT LABOR COSTS INCURRED
+ MANUFACTURING OVERHEAD APPLIED
- WORK-IN-PROCESS INVENTORY, ENDING
= COST OF GOODS MANUFACTURED

> COST OF GOODS SOLD:

FINISHED GOODS INVENTORY, BEGINNING
+ COST OF GOODS MANUFACTURED
- FINISHED GOODS INVENTORY, ENDING
= COST OF GOODS SOLD

RELATIONSHIP OF TOTAL COST TO VOLUME OF ACTIVITY

KEY IDEA

> **COST BEHAVIOR PATTERN** DESCRIBES HOW TOTAL COST VARIES WITH CHANGES IN ACTIVITY.

KEY RELATIONSHIPS

> VARIABLE COST

> FIXED COST

EXHIBIT 12–9 Cost Behavior Patterns

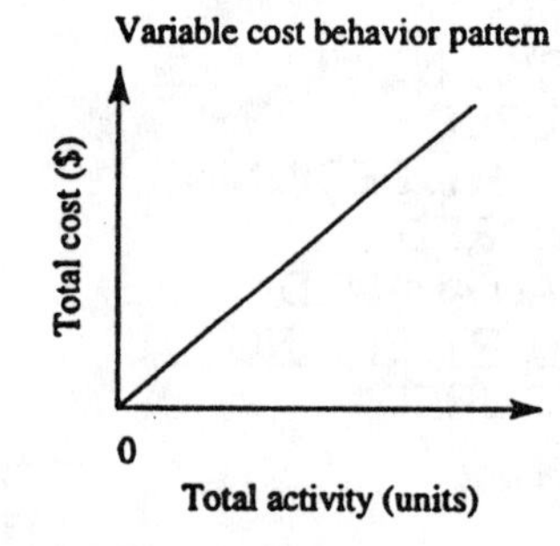

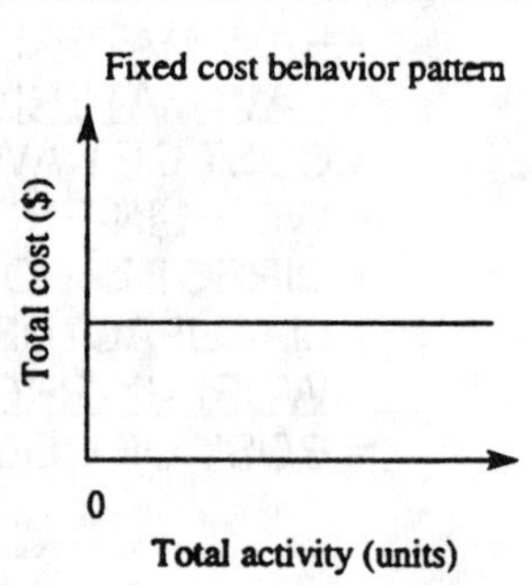

KEY ASSUMPTIONS

> RELEVANT RANGE

> LINEARITY

COST FORMULA

KEY POINT

> A **COST FORMULA** DESCRIBES THE EXPECTED TOTAL COST FOR ANY VOLUME OF ACTIVITY, USING COST BEHAVIOR INFORMATION.

KEY RELATIONSHIP

> TOTAL COST = FIXED COST + VARIABLE COST

= FIXED COST + (VARIABLE RATE PER UNIT X ACTIVITY)

KEY IDEA

> WHENEVER POSSIBLE, AVOID UNITIZING FIXED COSTS, BECAUSE THEY DO NOT BEHAVE THAT WAY!

ACTIVITY BASED COSTING

KEY POINT

> AN ABC SYSTEM INVOLVES IDENTIFYING THE KEY ACTIVITIES THAT CAUSE THE INCURRANCE OF COST; THESE ACTIVITIES ARE KNOWN AS **COST DRIVERS.**

> EXAMPLES OF COST DRIVERS INCLUDE: MACHINE SETUP, QUALITY INSPECTION, PRODUCTION ORDER PREPARATION, AND MATERIALS HANDLING ACTIVITIES.

KEY RELATIONSHIPS

> THE NUMBER OF TIMES EACH ACTIVITY IS TO BE PERFORMED DURING THE YEAR AND THE TOTAL COST OF EACH ACTIVITY ARE ESTIMATED, AND A PREDETERMINED COST PER ACTIVITY IS CALCULATED.

> "ACTIVITY BASED COSTS" ARE THEN APPLIED TO PRODUCTS, RATHER THAN USING A TRADITIONAL METHOD OF OVERHEAD APPLICATION SUCH AS DIRECT LABOR HOURS OR MACHINE HOURS.

KEY IDEA

> ABC SYSTEMS OFTEN LEAD TO MORE ACCURATE PRODUCT COSTING AND MORE EFFECTIVE COST CONTROL, BECAUSE MANAGEMENT'S ATTENTION IS DIRECTED TO THE ACTIVITIES THAT ***CAUSE*** THE INCURRANCE OF COST.

INCOME STATEMENT MODELS

TRADITIONAL MODEL

REVENUES
- COST OF GOODS SOLD
GROSS PROFIT
- OPERATING EXPENSES
OPERATING INCOME

CONTRIBUTION MARGIN MODEL

REVENUES
- VARIABLE EXPENSES
CONTRIBUTION MARGIN
- FIXED EXPENSES
OPERATING INCOME

KEY IDEAS

> THE TRADITIONAL MODEL CLASSIFIES EXPENSES BY FUNCTION, AND THE CONTRIBUTION MARGIN MODEL CLASSIFIES EXPENSES BY COST BEHAVIOR PATTERN.

> THE CONTRIBUTION MARGIN MODEL IS USEFUL FOR DETERMINING THE EFFECT ON OPERATING INCOME OF CHANGES IN THE LEVEL OF ACTIVITY.

EXPANDED CONTRIBUTION MARGIN MODEL

		PER UNIT	X	VOLUME	=	TOTAL	%
REVENUE	$	(1.)				$	100 %
VARIABLE EXP.		(1.)					
CONT. MARGIN	$	(1.)	X	(2.)	=	(2.)	
FIXED EXPENSES						$ (3.)	
OPERATING INCOME						$ (3.)	

KEY IDEAS

> THE PREFERRED ROUTE THROUGH THE MODEL IS:

(1.) TO ENTER PER UNIT REVENUE AND VARIABLE EXPENSES TO GET UNIT CONTRIBUTION MARGIN.

(2.) THEN MULTIPLY UNIT CONTRIBUTION MARGIN BY VOLUME (QUANTITY SOLD) TO GET TOTAL CONTRIBUTION MARGIN.

(3.) FIXED EXPENSES ARE NOT EXPRESSED ON A PER UNIT BASIS; THEY ARE SUBTRACTED FROM TOTAL CONTRIBUTION MARGIN TO GET OPERATING INCOME.

> THE CONTRIBUTION MARGIN RATIO EXPRESSES CONTRIBUTION MARGIN AS A PERCENTAGE OF REVENUES, ON EITHER A PER UNIT OR TOTAL BASIS.

BREAK-EVEN POINT ANALYSIS

KEY IDEA

> MANAGERS FREQUENTLY WANT TO KNOW THE NUMBER OF UNITS THAT MUST BE SOLD, OR THE TOTAL SALES DOLLARS REQUIRED, TO BREAK-EVEN (HAVE ZERO OPERATING INCOME).

BREAK-EVEN GRAPH

EXHIBIT 13–4 Break-Even Graph

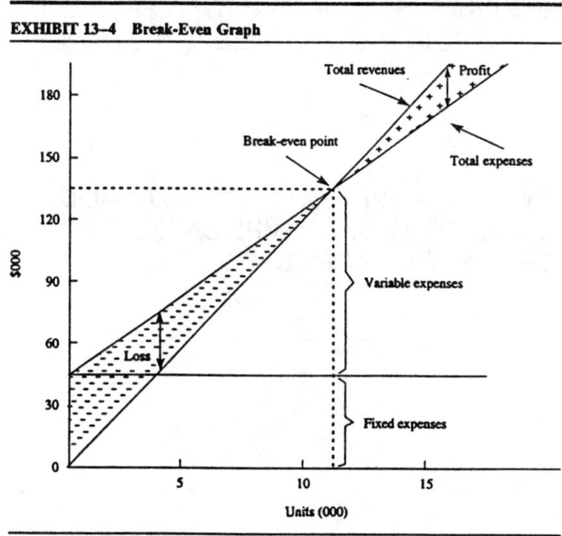

KEY POINT

> ONCE THE BREAK-EVEN POINT HAS BEEN REACHED, OPERATING INCOME INCREASES BY THE AMOUNT OF CONTRIBUTION MARGIN FROM EACH ADDITIONAL UNIT SOLD.

KEY ASSUMPTIONS TO REMEMBER WHEN USING CONTRIBUTION MARGIN ANALYSIS

> COST BEHAVIOR PATTERNS CAN BE IDENTIFIED.

> COSTS ARE LINEAR WITHIN THE RELEVANT RANGE.

> ACTIVITY REMAINS WITHIN THE RELEVANT RANGE.

> SALES MIX OF THE FIRM'S PRODUCTS WITH DIFFERENT CONTRIBUTION MARGIN RATIOS DOES NOT CHANGE.

KEY POINT

> IF THESE SIMPLIFYING ASSUMPTIONS ARE NOT VALID. THE ANALYSIS IS MADE MORE COMPLICATED BUT THE CONCEPTS ARE STILL APPLICABLE.

BUDGETING

BUDGET CATEGORIES

> OPERATING BUDGET

> CAPITAL BUDGET

APPROACHES TO BUDGETING

> TOP-DOWN

> PARTICIPATIVE

> ZERO-BASED

BUDGET TIME FRAMES

> SINGLE-PERIOD BUDGET

> ROLLING (CONTINUOUS) BUDGET

OPERATING BUDGET PREPARATION SEQUENCE

> SALES / REVENUE BUDGET, OR SALES FORECAST

> PURCHASES / PRODUCTION BUDGET

> OPERATING EXPENSE BUDGET

> BUDGETED INCOME STATEMENT

> CASH BUDGET

> BALANCE SHEET BUDGET

KEY POINT

> THE ENTIRE BUDGET BUILDS ON THE SALES/ REVENUE BUDGET, SOMETIMES CALLED THE SALES FORECAST.

PERFORMANCE REPORTING

KEY IDEAS

> IF TIME AND EFFORT HAVE BEEN EXPENDED PREPARING A BUDGET, IT IS APPROPRIATE TO COMPARE ACTUAL RESULTS WITH BUDGETED RESULTS. THIS IS DONE IN THE PERFORMANCE REPORT.

> IF ACTUAL RESULTS APPROXIMATE BUDGETED RESULTS, THEN NO SIGNIFICANT FURTHER EVALUATION OF PERFORMANCE NEEDS TO BE MADE.

MANAGEMENT ATTENTION IS GIVEN ONLY TO THOSE ACTIVITIES FOR WHICH ACTUAL RESULTS VARY SIGNIFICANTLY FROM BUDGETED RESULTS. THIS IS **MANAGEMENT BY EXCEPTION.**

SEGMENT REPORTING

KEY IDEAS

> WHEN A FIRM HAS SEVERAL IDENTIFIABLE SEGMENTS (DIVISIONS, SALES TERRITORIES, PRODUCTS, ETC.) MANAGEMENT FREQUENTLY WANTS TO EVALUATE THE OPERATING RESULTS OF EACH SEGMENT.

> SEGMENTS MAY BE REFERRED TO AS:

COST CENTERS

PROFIT CENTERS

INVESTMENT CENTERS

KEY ISSUES

> SALES, VARIABLE EXPENSES, AND CONTRIBUTION MARGIN FOR EACH SEGMENT CAN USUALLY BE EASILY ACCUMULATED FROM THE ACCOUNTING RECORDS.

> FIXED EXPENSES INCLUDE AMOUNTS ASSOCIATED DIRECTLY WITH EACH SEGMENT, AND AMOUNTS THAT ARE COMMON TO THE FIRM AS A WHOLE. TO REPORT SENSIBLE RESULTS FOR EACH SEGMENT, **COMMON FIXED EXPENSES SHOULD NEVER BE ARBITRARILY ALLOCATED TO THE SEGMENTS** BECAUSE THEY ARE NOT INCURRED DIRECTLY BY ANY OF THE SEGMENTS.

FLEXIBLE BUDGETING

KEY ISSUES

> BUDGET AMOUNTS ARE BASED ON EXPECTED LEVELS OF ACTIVITY. ACTUAL ACTIVITY IS UNLIKELY TO BE THE SAME AS BUDGETED ACTIVITY.

> SOME MANAGER IS RESPONSIBLE FOR THE DIFFERENCE BETWEEN BUDGETED AND ACTUAL ACTIVITY LEVELS, BUT IT IS USUALLY ANOTHER MANAGER WHO IS RESPONSIBLE FOR THE COSTS INCURRED.

> REVENUES ARE A FUNCTION OF UNITS SOLD, AND COSTS INCURRED ARE A FUNCTION OF COST BEHAVIOR PATTERNS.

KEY IDEA

> AT THE END OF A PERIOD, WHEN THE ACTUAL LEVEL OF ACTIVITY IS KNOWN, THE ORIGINAL BUDGET SHOULD BE **FLEXED** SO THAT THE PERFORMANCE REPORT COMPARES ACTUAL RESULTS WITH BUDGET AMOUNTS BASED ON ACTUAL ACTIVITY.

KEY POINT

> ONLY REVENUES AND VARIABLE EXPENSES ARE FLEXED. FIXED EXPENSES ARE NOT A FUNCTION OF THE LEVEL OF ACTIVITY (UNLESS ACTIVITY FALLS OUTSIDE OF THE RELEVANT RANGE).

STANDARD COSTS

WHAT ARE THEY?

> UNIT BUDGETS FOR MATERIALS, LABOR, AND OVERHEAD COST COMPONENTS OF A PRODUCT OR PROCESS.

> STANDARD COSTS ARE USED FOR PLANNING AND CONTROL.

KEY IDEAS

> STANDARD COSTS CAN BE BASED ON:

IDEAL, OR ENGINEERED, PERFORMANCE

ATTAINABLE PERFORMANCE

PAST EXPERIENCE

> THE STANDARD COST OF PRODUCT OR PROCESS COMPONENTS CAN BE USED TO BUILD UP THE TOTAL COST OF A PRODUCT OR PROCESS.

VARIABLE COST VARIANCE ANALYSIS

KEY IDEAS

> IT IS APPROPRIATE TO EVALUATE PERFORMANCE BY COMPARING ACTUAL COSTS WITH STANDARD COSTS, AND ANALYZING WHY ANY VARIANCES OCCURRED.

> THE REASON FOR CALCULATING VARIANCES IS TO ENCOURAGE ACTION TO ELIMINATE UNFAVORABLE VARIANCES AND CAPTURE FAVORABLE VARIANCES.

KEY POINTS

> VARIANCE TERMINOLOGY

INPUT	QUANTITY VARIANCE	COST PER UNIT OF INPUT VARIANCE
RAW MATERIALS	USAGE	PRICE
DIRECT LABOR	EFFICIENCY	RATE
VAR. OVERHEAD	EFFICIENCY	SPENDING

> DIFFERENT MANAGERS ARE USUALLY RESPONSIBLE FOR THE QUANTITY AND COST PER UNIT OF INPUT VARIANCES. THAT IS WHY THEY ARE CALCULATED AND REPORTED SEPARATELY.

> THE REPORTING OF VARIANCES SHOULD LEAD TO BETTER COMMUNICATION AND COORDINATION OF ACTIVITIES.

FIXED COST VARIANCE ANALYSIS

KEY ISSUE

> FOR MANY FIRMS, FIXED MANUFACTURING OVERHEAD HAS BECOME MORE SIGNIFICANT THAN VARIABLE MANUFACTURING COSTS. THEREFORE, MANY FIRMS ARE INCREASING EFFORTS TO CONTROL FIXED OVERHEAD.

KEY POINTS

> VARIANCE TERMINOLOGY

BUDGET VARIANCE IS THE DIFFERENCE BETWEEN BUDGETED FIXED OVERHEAD COSTS AND ACTUAL FIXED OVERHEAD COSTS.

VOLUME VARIANCE IS CAUSED BY THE DIFFERENCE BETWEEN THE PLANNED LEVEL OF ACTIVITY USED IN THE CALCULATION OF THE PREDETERMINED OVERHEAD APPLICATION RATE, AND THE ACTUAL LEVEL OF ACTIVITY.

> THE SUM OF THE BUDGET VARIANCE AND THE VOLUME VARIANCE EQUALS THE OVERAPPLIED OR UNDERAPPLIED FIXED MANUFACTURING OVERHEAD.

CAPITAL BUDGETING

WHAT'S GOING ON?

> PROPOSED CAPITAL EXPENDITURES USUALLY INVOLVE RETURNS RECEIVED OVER EXTENDED PERIODS OF TIME, SO IT IS APPROPRIATE TO RECOGNIZE THE TIME VALUE OF MONEY WHEN EVALUATING WHETHER OR NOT THE INVESTMENT WILL GENERATE THE DESIRED ROI.

KEY POINT

> PRESENT VALUE ANALYSIS RECOGNIZES THE TIME VALUE OF MONEY.

KEY ISSUES

> PRESENT VALUE ANALYSIS USES

THE INVESTMENT AMOUNT ----->
THE EXPECTED CASH RETURNS ----->
AND AN INTEREST RATE (COST OF CAPITAL) ---->

TO ANSWER THE FOLLOWING QUESTION:

IS THE PRESENT VALUE OF THE FUTURE CASH FLOWS FROM THE INVESTMENT, DISCOUNTED AT THE COST OF CAPITAL, AT LEAST EQUAL TO THE AMOUNT THAT MUST BE INVESTED?

IF THE ANSWER IS "YES", THEN THE ROI ON THE CAPITAL EXPENDITURE IS AT LEAST EQUAL TO THE COST OF CAPITAL, AND THE INVESTMENT SHOULD BE MADE.

CAPITAL BUDGETING ANALYSIS TECHNIQUES

METHODS THAT USE PRESENT VALUE ANALYSIS

> NET PRESENT VALUE (NPV) METHOD

GIVEN A COST OF CAPITAL, COMPUTE THE PRESENT VALUE OF THE CASH RETURNS FROM THE INVESTMENT AND THEN SUBTRACT THE INVESTMENT REQUIRED. THIS DIFFERENCE IS THE NET PRESENT VALUE (NPV) OF THE PROJECT.

IF THE NPV IS POSITIVE, ROI > COST OF CAPITAL, SO THE INVESTMENT SHOULD BE MADE.

IF THE NPV IS NEGATIVE, ROI < COST OF CAPITAL, SO THE INVESTMENT SHOULD NOT BE MADE.

IF THE NPV IS ZERO, ROI = COST OF CAPITAL, SO THE FIRM WOULD BE INDIFFERENT ABOUT THE INVESTMENT PROPOSAL.

> INTERNAL RATE OF RETURN (IRR) METHOD

SOLVE FOR THE INTEREST RATE AT WHICH THE PRESENT VALUE OF THE CASH RETURNS EQUALS THE INVESTMENT REQUIRED. THIS IS THE PROPOSED INVESTMENT'S ROI - REFERRED TO AS THE INTERNAL RATE OF RETURN (IRR).

THE INVESTMENT DECISION IS MADE BASED ON THE RELATIONSHIP BETWEEN THE PROJECT'S INTERNAL RATE OF RETURN (IRR) AND THE FIRM'S DESIRED ROI (COST OF CAPITAL).

CAPITAL BUDGETING ANALYSIS TECHNIQUES

METHODS THAT DO NOT USE PRESENT VALUE ANALYSIS

> PAYBACK METHOD

HOW LONG DOES IT TAKE FOR THE CASH FLOWS TO EQUAL THE AMOUNT OF THE INVESTMENT?

> ACCOUNTING RATE OF RETURN METHOD

WHAT IS THE ROI BASED ON FINANCIAL STATEMENT REPORTING OF THE INVESTMENT AND OPERATING RESULTS?

KEY ISSUE

> EACH OF THESE METHODS IS SIGNIFICANTLY FLAWED BECAUSE EACH IGNORES THE TIME VALUE OF MONEY.

Solutions to Odd-Numbered Problems

Chapter 1. Accounting: Past and Present

1-5. The principal factors John Hall must consider are his competence and independence. Is he competent to prepare financial statements for a company that operates in a different industry than the one in which he works? A contingent fee arrangement would be considered an impairment of his independence because he would directly benefit if the loan is approved.

Chapter 2. Financial Statements and Accounting Concepts/Principles

2-1.

	Category	*Financial Statement(s)*
Cash	A	BS
Accounts payable	L	BS
Common stock	OE	BS, SOE
Depreciation expense	E	IS
Net sales	R	IS
Income tax expense	E	IS
Short-term investments	A	BS
Gain on sale of land	G	IS
Retained earnings	OE	BS, SOE
Dividends payable	L	BS
Accounts receivable	A	BS
Short-term debt	L	BS

2-3. Use the accounting equation to solve for the missing information.

Firm A:

A	=	L	+	PIC	+ (Beg. RE	+	NI	−	DIV	=	End. RE)
$420,000	=	$215,000	+	$75,000	+ ($78,000	+	?	−	$50,000	=	?)

In this case, the ending balance of retained earnings must be determined first:
$420,000 = $215,000 + $75,000 + End. RE.
Retained earnings, 12/31/96 = **$130,000.**

Once the ending balance of retained earnings is known, net income can be determined:
$78,000 + NI – $50,000 = $130,000.
Net income for 1996 = **$102,000.**

2-3. Firm B:

A	=	L	+	PIC	+(Beg. RE +	NI	–	DIV	= End. RE)
$540,000	=	$145,000	+	?	+(?	+$83,000	–	$19,000	= $310,000)

$540,000 = $145,000 + PIC + $310,000
Paid-in capital, 12/31/96 = **$85,000.**

Beg. RE + $83,000 – $19,000 = $310,000
Retained earnings, 1/1/96 = **$246,000.**

Firm C:

A	=	L	+	PIC	+ (Beg. RE +	NI	–	DIV	= End. RE)
$325,000	=	?	+	$40,000	+ ($42,000 +	$113,000	–	$65,000	= ?)

In this case, the ending balance of retained earnings must be determined first:
$42,000 + $113,000 – $65,000 = End. RE
Retained earnings, 12/31/96 = **$90,000.**

Once the ending balance of retained earnings is known, liabilities can be determined:
$325,000 = L + $40,000 + $90,000.
Total liabilities, 12/31/96 = **$195,000.**

2-5. Prepare the retained earning portion of a statement of changes in owners' equity for the year ended December 31, 1996:

Retained earnings, December 31, 1995	$230,700
Less: Net loss for the year ended December 31, 1996	(12,200)
Less: Dividends declared and paid in 1996	(8,000)
Retained earnings, December 31, 1996	**$210,500**

2-7.

					OE		
	A	**=**	**L**	**+**	**PIC**	**+**	**RE**
Beginning:	12	=	7	+	0	+	5
Changes:			–1				+3 (net income)
							? (dividends)
Ending:	?	=	?	+	0	+	6

2-7. ***Solution approach:*** (Remember that **net assets** = Assets – Liabilities = Owners' equity = PIC + RE). Since paid-in capital did not change during the year, assume that the beginning and ending balances are $0. Thus, beginning retained earnings = $12 – $7 = $5, and ending retained earnings = net assets at the end of the year = $6. By looking at the RE column, it can be seen that **dividends** must have been **$2.** Also by looking at the liabilities column, it can be seen that ending liabilities are $6, and therefore ending assets must be $12. Thus, total assets did not change during the year.

2-9. Set up the accounting equation and show the effects of the transactions described. Since total assets must equal total liabilities and owners' equity, the *unadjusted* owners' equity can be calculated by subtracting liabilities from the total of the assets given.

	A							=	L	+	OE
	Cash	+	Inventory	+	Accounts Receivable	+	Plant & Equipment	=	Liabilities	+	Owners' Equity
Data given	$ 22,800	+	61,400	+	114,200	+	265,000	=	305,600	+	157,800
Liquidation of inventory *	+49,120		-61,400								-12,280
Collection of acc. rec. *	+108,490				-114,200						-5,710
Sale of plant & equipment *	+190,000						-265,000				-75,000
Payment of liabilities	-305,600								-305,600		
Balance	**$ 64,810**	+	0	+	0	+	0	=	0	+	**$ 64,810**

* The effects of these transactions on owners' equity represent losses from the sale (or collection) of the non-cash assets.

2-11. a.

Accounts receivable	$ 33,000
Cash	9,000
Supplies	6,000
Merchandise inventory	31,000
Total current assets	**$ 79,000**

2-11. b.

Accounts payable	$ 23,000
Long-term debt	40,000
Common stock	10,000
Retained earnings	59,000
Total liabilities and owners' equity	**$132,000**

c.

Service revenue	$ 70,000
Depreciation expense	(12,000)
Supplies expense	(14,000)
Earnings from operations (operating income)	**$ 44,000**

d.

Earnings from operations (operating income)	$ 44,000
Interest expense	(4,000)
Earnings before taxes	$ 40,000
Income tax expense	(12,000)
Net income	**$ 28,000**

e. $12,000 income tax expense / $40,000 earnings before taxes = **30% tax rate.**

f.

Retained earnings, January 1, 1996	?
Net income for the year	$ 28,000
Dividends declared and paid during the year	(16,000)
Retained earnings, December 31, 1996	$ 59,000

Solving the model, the beginning retained earnings balance must have been **$47,000**, because the account balance increased by $12,000, to an ending balance of $59,000.

2-13. a.

BREANNA, INC.
Income Statement
For the Year Ended December 31, 1996

Sales	$200,000
Cost of goods sold	(128,000)
Gross profit	$ 72,000
Selling, general, and administrative expenses	(34,000)
Earnings from operations (operating income)	$ 38,000
Interest expense	(6,000)
Earnings before taxes	$ 32,000
Income tax expense	(8,000)
Net income	$ 24,000

2-13. a. ***(Continued)***

BREANNA, INC.
Statement of Changes in Owners' Equity
For the Year Ended December 31, 1996

Paid-in capital:		
Common stock		$ 90,000
Retained earnings:		
Beginning balance	$ 23,000	
Net income for the year	24,000	
Less: Dividends declared and paid during the year	(12,000)	
Ending balance		35,000
Total owners' equity		$125,000

BREANNA, INC.
Balance Sheet
December 31, 1996

Assets:		
Cash	$ 65,000	
Accounts receivable	10,000	
Merchandise inventory	37,000	
Total current assets		$112,000
Equipment	120,000	
Less: Accumulated depreciation	(52,000)	68,000
Total assets		$180,000
Liabilities:		
Accounts payable	$ 15,000	
Long-term debt	40,000	
Total liabilities		$ 55,000
Owners' Equity:		
Common stock	$ 90,000	
Retained earnings	35,000	
Total owners' equity		$125,000
Total liabilities and owners' equity		$180,000

b. $8,000 income tax expense / $32,000 earnings before taxes = **25% tax rate.**

c. $6,000 interest expense / $40,000 long-term debt = **15% interest rate.** This assumes that the year-end balance of long-term debt is representative of the *average* long-term debt account balance throughout the year.

d. $90,000 common stock / 9,000 shares = **$10 per share par value.**

e. $12,000 dividends declared and paid/ $24,000 net income = **50%.** This assumes that the board of directors has a policy to pay dividends in proportion to earnings.

2-15. a.

Retained earnings, January 1, 1997	$ 75,000
Net income for the year	?
Dividends declared and paid during the year	(17,000)
Retained earnings, December 31, 1997	$ 70,000

Solving for the missing amount, **net income** for the year is **$12,000.**

Revenues	$120,000
Expenses	?
Net income	$ 12,000

Solving for the missing amount, **total expenses** for the year are **$108,000.**

b.

GARBER, INC.
Statement of Cash Flows
For the Year Ended December 31, 1997

Cash flows from operating activities	$ 27,000
Cash flows from investing activities	0
Cash flows from financing activities #	(12,000)
Net increase in cash for the year	$ 15,000
Cash balance, January 1, 1997	35,000
Cash balance, December 31, 1997	$ 50,000

Notes payable ($5,000), Dividends ($17,000), Common Stock $10,000.

c. Depreciation expense of $15,000 was added back to net income to arrive at the cash flows from operating activities. (Since no production equipment was purchased or sold during the year, the $15,000 decrease in net production equipment is attributable to depreciation expense.)

d. Garber, Inc., is better off at the end of the year. Although total assets did not change during the year, liabilities decreased by $5,000 and total owners' equity increased by $5,000. Net income of $12,000 was earned, and this is the bottom-line measure of profitability. In addition, the firm generated $27,000 in cash flows from operations and $10,000 from the sale of common stock (a financing activity). These cash flows allowed Garber, Inc., to reduce its long-term debt by $5,000, pay dividends of $17,000, and still have a net increase in cash of $15,000.

2-17.

	Assets =	*Liabilities* +	*Owners' Equity*
a. Borrowed cash on a bank loan	+	+	NE
b. Paid an account payable	–	–	NE
c. Sold common stock	+	NE	+
d. Purchased merchandise inventory on account	+	+	NE
e. Paid dividends	–	NE	–
f. Collected an account receivable	NE	NE	NE
g. Sold inventory on account at a profit	+	NE	+
h. Paid operating expenses in cash	–	NE	–
i. Repaid principal and interest on a bank loan	–	–	–

2-19. Amounts shown in the balance sheet below reflect the following use of the data given:

a. An asset should have a "probable future economic benefit"; therefore the accounts receivable are stated at the amount expected to be collected from customers.

b. Assets are reported at original cost, not current "worth." Depreciation in accounting reflects the spreading of the cost of an asset over its estimated useful life.

c. Assets are reported at original cost, not at an assessed or appraised value.

d. The amount of the note payable is calculated using the accounting equation, A = L + OE. Total assets can be determined based on items (a), (b), and (c); total owners' equity is known after considering item (e); and the note payable is the difference between total liabilities and the accounts payable.

e. Retained earnings is the difference between cumulative net income and cumulative dividends.

Assets:			**Liabilities and Owners' Equity:**		
Cash		$ 700	Note payable	$ 2,200	
Accounts receivable		3,400	Accounts payable	3,400	
Land		7,000	Total liabilities		$ 5,600
Automobile	$9,000		Capital stock	8,000	
Less: Accumulated depreciation	(3,000)	6,000	Retained earnings	3,500	
			Total owners' equity		11,500
Total assets		$17,100	Total liabilities and owners' equity		$17,100

2-21. ***Solution approach:*** The strategy is to enter the amount of the *change* for each asset, liability and owners' equity item between the two dates. Each of these changes will be used in the Statement of Cash Flows. (*Note*: Because the retained earnings section of the balance sheet is, in and of itself, an analysis of the change in the retained earnings account for the month, *total net income* and *total dividends* for the month of February are shown as changes).

2-21. *(Continued)*

MILLCO, INC.
Balance Sheets
January 31 and February 28, 1997

	Feb. 28	*Jan. 31*	*Change*
Assets:			
Cash	$ 42,000	$ 37,000	+5,000
Accounts receivable	64,000	53,000	+11,000
Merchandise inventory	81,000	94,000	−13,000
Total current assets	$187,000	$184,000	
Plant and Equipment:			
Production equipment	166,000	152,000	+14,000
Less: Accumulated depreciation	(24,000)	(21,000)	+(3,000)
Total assets	$329,000	$315,000	
Liabilities:			
Short-term debt	$ 44,000	$ 44,000	0
Accounts payable	37,000	41,000	− 4,000
Other accrued liabilities	21,000	24,000	− 3,000
Total current liabilities	$102,000	$109,000	
Long-term debt	33,000	46,000	−13,000
Total liabilities	$135,000	$155,000	
Owners' Equity:			
Common stock, no par value, 40,000 shares authorized, 30,000 and 20,000 shares issued, respectively	$104,000	$ 96,000	+8,000
Retained earnings:			
Beginning balance	$ 64,000	$ 43,000	
Net income for the month	36,000	29,000	+36,000
Dividends	(10,000)	(8,000)	−10,000
Ending balance	$ 90,000	$ 64,000	
Total owners' equity	$ 194,000	$160,000	
Total liabilities and owners' equity	$ 329,000	$315,000	

2-21. ***(Continued)***
The statement of cash flows uses the changes between the two month-end balance sheets, as illustrated below:

MILLCO, INC.
Statement of Cash Flows
For the Month Ended February 28, 1997

Cash flows from operating activities:		
Net income	$ 36,000	
Add (deduct) items not affecting cash:		
Depreciation expense	3,000	
Increase in accounts receivable	(11,000)	
Decrease in merchandise inventory	13,000	
Decrease in accounts payable	(4,000)	
Decrease in other accrued liabilities	(3,000)	
Net cash provided by operating activities		34,000
Cash flows from investing activities:		
Purchases of production equipment		(14,000)
Cash flows from financing activities:		
Payment of long-term debt	$(13,000)	
Sale of common stock	8,000	
Payment of dividends	(10,000)	
Net cash flows used by financing activities		$(15,000)
Net increase in cash for the year		$ 5,000

Notice that the statement of cash flows has explained the +$5,000 change in cash during the year by using the change in every other balance sheet item.

2-23. a.

HARRIS, INC.
Balance Sheet
December 31, 1996

Assets

Current assets:		
Cash	$ 6,000	
Accounts receivable	67,000	
Merchandise inventory	46,000	
Total current assets		$ 119,000

2-23. a.

Total current assets		$ 119,000
Noncurrent assets:		
Land	27,000	
Buildings	208,000	
Less: Accumulated depreciation	(101,000)	
Total noncurrent assets		134,000
Total assets		$ 253,000

Liabilities and Owners' Equity

Current liabilities:		
Short-term debt	$ 12,000	
Notes payable	24,000	
Accounts payable	61,000	
Total current liabilities		$ 97,000
Long-term debt		65,000
Owners' equity:		
Common stock, no par	$ 28,000	
Retained earnings	63,000	
Total owners' equity		91,000
Total liabilities and owners' equity		$ 253,000

b.

HARRIS, INC.
Statement of Changes in Retained Earnings
For the Year Ended December 31, 1996

Retained earnings, 1/1/96	$ 55,000
Add: Net income for the year	13,000
Less: Dividends for the year	(5,000)
Retained earnings balance 12/31/96	$ 63,000

2-25. If students are willing to share the different kinds of assets they have identified, this problem can be used to review the characteristics of assets.

Chapter 3. Fundamental Interpretations Made from Financial Statement Data

3-1. a. ROI = (Amount of return / Amount invested)
Julie = ($50 / $560) = **8.93%.** Sam = ($53 / $620) = **8.55%**

b. Risk is a principal factor to be considered.

3-3. ***Solution approach:*** Calculate the amount of return from each alternative, then calculate the ROI of the additional return from the higher paying investment relative to the $50 that must be invested to get the higher return.

ROI * amount invested = amount of return.
Alternative # 1 10% * $500 = **$50 return.**
Alternative # 2 10.5% * $550 = **$57.75 return.**

The extra amount of return of $7.75 on an additional investment of $50 is an ROI of 15.5%. **($7.75 / $50 = 15.5%).** Therefore, do not pay an interest rate of more than 15.5% to borrow the additional $50 needed for the higher yield investment.

3-5. The following model can be used to help answer any questions related to ROI:

ROI	=	MARGIN	x	TURNOVER
NET INCOME / AVERAGE TOTAL ASSETS	=	NET INCOME / SALES	x	SALES / AVERAGE TOTAL ASSETS

a. 18% ROI = 12% Margin * ($600,000 Sales / Average total assets)
Average total assets = **$400,000**

b. ROI = ($78,000 Net income / $950,000 Average total assets) = **8.21%**

or: 1.3 Turnover = (Sales / $950,000 Average total assets)
Sales = **$1,235,000**

ROI = ($78,000 Net income / $1,235,000 Sales) * 1.3 Turnover
ROI = (6.32% Margin * 1.3 Turnover) = **8.21%**

c. 7.37% ROI = (Margin * 2.1 Turnover)
Margin = **3.5%**

3-7. Remember that "net assets" is the same as "owners' equity."

Beginning net assets	$346,800
Add: Net income	42,300
Less: Dividends	(12,000)
Ending net assets	$377,100

ROE = Net income / Average owners' equity
= $42,300 / (($346,800 + $377,100) / 2) = **11.7%**

3-9. a. ROI = (32% Margin * 0.4 Turnover) = **12.8%**
0.4 Turnover = (Sales / $800,000 Average total assets)
Sales = **$320,000**

b. 12.8% ROI = (15% Margin * Turnover)
Turnover = **0.85333**
0.85333 Turnover = (Sales / $800,000 Average total assets)
Sales = **$682,664**

3-11. a. ROI = Margin * Turnover
= (Net earnings / Sales) * (Sales / Average total assets)
= ($210.4 / $2,752.7) * ($2,752.7 / (($1,929.3 + $2,232.5) / 2))
= (7.6% Margin * 1.32 Turnover) = **10.1%**

b. ROE = Net income / Average owners' equity
= $210.4 / (($569.5 + 735.1) / 2) = **32.3%**

c. Working capital = Current assets – Current liabilities

	12/31/94	*12/31/93*
Current assets	$ 691.0	$ 640.4
– Current liabilities	(387.3)	(436.3)
= Working capital	**$ 303.7**	**$ 204.1**

d. Current ratio = Current assets / Current liabilities

	12/31/94	*12/31/93*
Current assets	$ 691.0	$ 640.4
/ Current liabilities	387.3	436.3
= Current ratio	**1.78**	**1.47**

e. Acid-test ratio = (Cash + Short-term securities + Accounts and Notes receivable) / Current liabilities

	12/31/94	*12/31/93*
Cash and cash equivalents	$ 12.0	$ 9.1
Accounts and notes receivable	320.0	283.5
Total (quick assets)	$332.0	$292.6

	12/31/94	*12/31/93*
Total (quick assets)	$332.0	$292.6
/ Current liabilities	$387.3	$436.3
= Acid-test ratio	**0.86**	**0.67**

3-13. a. ROI = Margin * Turnover
= (Net income / Sales) * (Sales / Average total assets)
= ($34,000 / $580,000) * (($580,000 / ($280,000 + $312,000)/2)
= (5.86% Margin * 1.959 Turnover) = **11.5%**

b. ROE = Net income / Average owners' equity
= $34,000 / (($167,000 + $196,000) / 2) = **18.7%**

c. Working capital = $202,000 Current assets – $94,000 Current liabilities = **$108,000**

d. Current ratio = ($202,000 Current assets / $94,000 Current liabilities) = **2.15**

e. Acid test ratio = (Cash + Accounts receivable) / Current liabilities
= ($21,000 + $78,000) / $94,000 = **1.05**

3-15. a. Working capital = Current assets – Current liabilities

	1/31/96	*1/31/95*
Current assets	$ 14	$ 18
– Current liabilities	(9)	(6)
= Working capital	**$ 5**	**$ 12**

Current ratio = Current assets / Current liabilities

	1/31/96	*1/31/95*
Current assets	$ 14	$ 18
/ Current liabilities	9	6
= Current ratio	**1.56**	**3.0**

b. Even though the firm has more cash at January 31, 1996, it is less liquid based on the working capital and current ratio measures. The firm owes more on accounts payable, and has less inventory to sell and fewer accounts receivable to collect, as compared to January 31, 1995.

c. Accounts receivable were collected, inventories were reduced, and current liabilities increased. These changes and the increase in cash are all possible, because changes in a firm's cash position and its profitability are not directly related.

3-17. a.

	Do Not Prepay Accounts Payable	*Prepay Accounts Payable*
Current assets	$ 12,639	$ 8,789
– Current liabilities	(7,480)	(3,630)
= Working capital	**$ 5,159**	**$ 5,159**
Current ratio	**1.69**	**2.42**

3-17. a. ***(Continued)***

Payment of the accounts payable does not affect working capital, but does improve the current ratio. Is this balance sheet "window dressing" worth the opportunity cost of not being able to invest the cash? Remember, once the payment is made, the cash is in someone else's hands.

b.

	Without Loan	*With Loan*
Current assets	$ 12,639	$ 17,639
- Current liabilities	(7,480)	(12,480)
= Working capital	**$ 5,159**	**$ 5,159**
Current ratio	**1.69**	**1.41**

If the loan is taken after the end of the fiscal year, the current ratio on the year-end balance sheet will be higher than if the loan is taken before the end of the year. Working capital is not affected. Thus, it makes sense to wait until after the end of the year to borrow on a short-term basis, unless cash is needed immediately.

Chapter 4. The Bookkeeping Process and Transaction Analysis

4-1.

	ASSETS				=	LIABILITIES	+	OWNERS' EQUITY	
Trans-action	Cash +	Accounts Receivable +	Merchandise Inventory +	Equipment =	Notes Payable +	Accounts Payable +	Paid-in Capital +	Revenues –	Expenses
a.	+ 180						+ 180		
b.	+ 100				+ 100				
c.	- 75			+ 75					
d.	- 40								- 40
e.	- 90		+ 150			+ 60			
f.	+ 65		- 40					+ 65	- 40
g.						+ 20			- 20
h.	- 120		+ 400			+ 280			
i.	+ 130	+ 320	- 300					+ 450	- 300
j.						+ 35*			- 35
Totals	150 +	320 +	210 +	75 =	100 +	395 +	180 +	515 -	435

Month-end totals: **Assets $755 = Liabilities $495 + Owners' equity $260**

Net income for the month: **Revenues $515 – Expenses $435 = Net income $80**

* Ordinarily, the Wages Payable account would be increased for employee wage expense that has been incurred but not yet paid.

4-3.

		Debit	Credit
a.	Dr. Cash	$180	
	Cr. Paid-In Capital		$180
b.	Dr. Cash	$100	
	Cr. Note Payable		$100
c.	Dr. Equipment	$75	
	Cr. Cash		$75
d.	Dr. Rent Expense	$40	
	Cr. Cash		$40
e.	Dr. Merchandise Inventory	$150	
	Cr. Cash		$90
	Cr. Accounts Payable		60
f.	Dr. Cash	$65	
	Cr. Sales Revenue		$65
	Dr. Cost of Goods Sold	$40	
	Cr. Merchandise Inventory		$40
g.	Dr. Advertising Expense	$20	
	Cr. Accounts Payable		$20
h.	Dr. Merchandise Inventory	$400	
	Cr. Cash		$120
	Cr. Accounts Payable		280
i.	Dr. Cash	$130	
	Dr. Accounts Receivable	320	
	Cr. Sales Revenue		$450
	Dr. Cost of Goods Sold	$300	
	Cr. Merchandise Inventory		$300
j.	Dr. Wages Expense	$35	
	Cr. Accounts (or Wages) Payable		$35

4-5.

Transaction/Situation	*Assets*	*Liabilities*	*Owners' Equity*	*Net Income*
a. Example transaction.	Supplies – 1,400			Supplies Exp – 1,400
b. Paid an insurance premium of $480 for the coming year. An asset, prepaid insurance, was debited	Prepaid Insurance + 480 Cash – 480			
c. Paid $3,200 of wages for the current month	Cash – 3,200			Wages Exp – 3,200

4-5. *(Continued)*

Transaction/Situation	*Assets*	*Liabilities*	*Owners' Equity*	*Net Income*
d. Received $250 of interest income for the current month	Cash + 250			Interest Inc + 250
e. Accrued $700 of commissions payable to sales staff for the current month		Commissions Payable + 700		Commissions Expense - 700
f. Accrued $130 of interest expense at the end of the month		Interest Pay + 130		Interest Exp - 130
g. Received $2,100 on accounts receivable accrued at the end of the prior month	Cash + 2,100 Accounts Rec - 2,100			
h. Purchased $600 of merchandise inventory from a supplier on account	Merch Inventory + 600	Accounts Payable + 600		
i. Paid $160 of interest expense for the month	Cash - 160			Interest Exp - 160
j. Accrued $800 of wages at the end of the current month		Wages Pay + 800		Wages Exp - 800
k. Paid $650 of accounts payable	Cash - 650	Accounts Pay - 650		

4-7.

Transaction/Situation	*Assets*	*Liabilities*	*Owners' Equity*	*Net Income*
a. Example transaction.	+ 550			+ 550
b. Paid an insurance premium of $360 for the coming year. An asset, "prepaid insurance" was debited	Cash – 360 Prepaid Insurance + 360			
c. Recognized insurance for one month from the above premium via a reclassification adjusting entry	Prepaid Insurance - 30			Insurance Expense - 30

4-7. *(Continued)*

Transaction/Situation	*Assets*	*Liabilities*	*Owners' Equity*	*Net Income*
d. Paid $800 of wages accrued at the end of the prior month	Cash – 800	Wages Payable – 800		
e. Paid $2,600 of wages for the current month	Cash – 2,600			Wages Exp – 2,600
f. Accrued $600 of wages at the end of the current month		Wages Payable + 600		Wages Exp – 600
g. Received cash of $1,500 on accounts receivable accrued at the end of the prior month	Cash +1,500 Accounts Rec – 1,500			

4-9.

		Debit	Credit
a.	Dr. Cash	$1,000,000	
	Cr. Common Stock		$1,000,000
b.	Dr. Cash	$500,000	
	Cr. Notes Payable		$500,000
c.	Dr. Salaries Expense	$380,000	
	Cr. Cash		$380,000
d.	Dr. Merchandise Inventory	$640,000	
	Cr. Accounts Payable		$640,000
e.	Dr. Accounts Receivable	$910,000	
	Cr. Sales		$910,000
	Dr. Cost of Goods Sold	$580,000	
	Cr. Merchandise Inventory		$580,000
f.	Dr. Rent Expense	$110,000	
	Cr. Cash		$110,000
g.	Dr. Equipment	$150,000	
	Cr. Cash		$ 50,000
	Cr. Accounts Payable		100,000
h.	Dr. Accounts Payable	$720,000	
	Cr. Cash		$720,000
i.	Dr. Utilities Expense	$36,000	
	Cr. Cash		$36,000
j.	Dr. Cash	$825,000	
	Cr. Accounts Receivable		$825,000
k.	Dr. Interest Expense	$60,000	
	Cr. Interest Payable		$60,000
l.	Dr. Rent Expense	$10,000	
	Cr. Rent Payable (or Accounts Payable)		$10,000

4-9. ***(Continued)***

	Balance Sheet			Income Statement		
	Assets =	Liabilities +	Owners' Equity <--	Net income =	Revenues -	Expenses
a.	Cash + 1,000,000		Common Stock + 1,000,000			
b.	Cash + 500,000	Notes Payable + 500,000				
c.	Cash - 380,000					Salaries Exp - 380,000
d.	Merchandise Inventory + 640,000	Accounts Payable + 640,000				
e.	Accounts Rec + 910,000 Merchandise Inv - 580,000				Sales + 910,000	Cost of Goods Sold - 580,000
f.	Cash - 110,000					Rent Exp - 110,000
g.	Equipment + 150,000 Cash - 50,000	Accounts Payable + 100,000				
h.	Cash - 720,000	Accounts Payable - 720,000				
i.	Cash - 36,000					Utilities Exp - 36,000
j.	Cash + 825,000 Accounts Rec - 825,000					
k.		Interest Pay + 60,000				Interest Exp - 60,000
l.		Rent Payable (or Accounts Pay) + 10,000				Rent Exp - 10,000

4-11. Prepare an analysis of the change in stockholders' equity for the month, showing the effects of the net loss and dividends:

Balance, February 1, 1996		$ 630,000
Revenues	$123,000	
Expenses	(131,000)	(8,000)
Dividends		(12,000)
Balance, February 28, 1996		**$ 610,000**

4-13.

Net sales	$741,000
Cost of goods sold	(329,000)
Gross profit	412,000
General and administrative expenses	(83,000)
Advertising expense	(76,000)
Other selling expenses	(42,000)
Earnings from operations (operating income)	**$211,000**

4-15. a. *4/1/96*

Dr. Note Receivable	$6,000	
Cr. Accounts Receivable		$6,000

b. *12/31/96*

Dr. Interest Receivable	$675	
Cr. Interest Revenue ($6,000 * 15% * 9/12)		$675

c. *3/31/97*

Dr. Cash	$6,900	
Cr. Note Receivable		$6,000
Cr. Interest Receivable		675
Cr. Interest Revenue		225

In entry *c*, only $675 of the total interest of $900 had been accrued, so the Interest Receivable account is reduced by the $675 that had been accrued in 1996; the other $225 that is received is recorded as interest revenue for 1997, the year in which it was earned.

Balance Sheet					Income Statement				
Assets	=	Liabilities	+	Owners' Equity	<-- Net income	=	Revenues	-	Expenses

a. *Receipt of note on April 1, 1996*:

Notes Receivable
+ 6,000
Account Receivable
– 6,000

4-15. ***(Continued)***

Balance Sheet						Income Statement				
Assets	=	Liabilities	+	Owners' Equity	<--	Net income	=	Revenues	–	Expenses

b. *Accrual of 9 month's interest at December 31, 1996*:

Assets	Revenues
Interest Receivable + 675	Interest Revenue + 675

c. *Collection of note and interest at March 31, 1997*:

Assets	Revenues
Cash + 6,900	Interest Revenue + 225
Note Receivable – 6,000	
Interest Receivable – 675	

4-17. a. *1/10/96*

	Dr.	Cr.
Dr. Paper Napkin Expense (or Supplies Expense)	$4,800	
Cr. Cash		$4,800

To record as an expense the cost of paper napkins purchased for cash.

b. *1/31/96*

	Dr.	Cr.
Dr. Paper Napkins on Hand (or Supplies)	$3,850	
Cr. Paper Napkin Expense (or Supplies Expense)		$3,850

To remove from the expense account and set up as an asset the cost of paper napkins on hand January 31.

c. *1/10/96*

	Dr.	Cr.
Dr. Paper Napkins on Hand (or Supplies)	$4,800	
Cr. Cash		$4,800

To set up as an asset the cost of paper napkins purchased for cash.

d. *1/31/96*

	Dr.	Cr.
Dr. Paper Napkin Expense (or Supplies Expense)	$950	
Cr. Paper Napkins on Hand (or Supplies)		$950

To record the cost of paper napkins used in January.

4-17. *(Continued)*

Balance Sheet					Income Statement				
Assets	=	Liabilities	+	Owners' Equity <--	Net income	=	Revenues	-	Expenses

a. *1/10/96. Record as an expense the cost of paper napkins purchased for cash:*

Assets	Expenses
Cash - 4,800	Supplies Expense - 4,800

b. *1/31/96. Remove from the expense account and set up as an asset the cost of the paper napkins on hand January 31.*

Assets		Expenses
Supplies + 3,850	*(Note: A reduction in Supplies Expense.)*	Supplies Expense + 3,850

c. *1/10/96. Set up as an asset the cost of paper napkins purchased for cash.*

Supplies
+ 4,800
Cash
- 4,800

d. *1/31/96. Record the cost of paper napkins used in January.*

Assets	Expenses
Supplies - 950	Supplies Expense - 950

e. Each approach results in the same expense for January and the same asset amount reported on the January 31 balance sheet.

4-19.

BIG BLUE RENTAL CORP.
Income Statement—August 1996

		Adjustments / Corrections		
	Preliminary	*Debit*	*Credit*	*Final*
Commission revenue	$ 4,500	$	$a) 200	$ 4,700
Interest revenue	850		f) 140	990
Total revenues	$ 5,350	$	$ 340	$ 5,690
Rent expense	$ 510	$	$e) 340	$ 170
Wages expense	1,190	d) 130		1,320
Supplies expense	--	b) 180		180
Interest expense	--	c) 20		20
Total expenses	$ 1,700	$ 330	$ 340	$ 1,690
Net income	$ 3,650	$ 330	$ 680	$ 4,000

4-19. *(Continued)*

BIG BLUE RENTAL CORP.		*Adjustments / Corrections*		
Balance Sheet—August 31, 1996	*Preliminary*	*Debit*	*Credit*	*Final*
Cash	$ 400	$	$	$ 400
Notes receivable	13,000			13,000
Commissions receivable	--	**a) 200**		200
Interest receivable	--	**f) 140**		140
Prepaid rent	--	**e) 340**		340
Supplies	650		**b) 180**	470
Total assets	$ 14,050	$ 680	$ 180	$14,550
Accounts payable	$ 120	$	$	$ 120
Note payable	2,400			2,400
Interest payable	40		**c) 20**	60
Wages payable	--		**d) 130**	130
Dividend payable	--		**g) 1,400**	1,400
Total liabilities	$ 2,560	$	$ 1,550	$ 4,110
Paid-in capital	$ 2,400	$	$	$ 2,400
Retained earnings:				
Balance, August 1	$ 5,440	$	$	$ 5,440
Net income	3,650	330	680	4,000
Dividends	--	**g) 1,400**		(1,400)
Balance, August 31	$ 9,090	$ 1,730	$ 680	$ 8,040
Total owners' equity	$ 11,490	$ 1,730	$ 680	$10,440
Total liabilities and owners' equity	$ 14,050	$ 1,730	$ 2,230	$14,550

Note: The net income line from the income statement is transferred down to the retained earnings section of the balance sheet. Remember, net income increases retained earnings, and net income is the link between the income statement and balance sheet. **This is an excellent study/review problem because it requires an understanding of much of the material that has been presented to this point in the course.**

Calculation for part c:
$2,400 Notes payable * 10% interest rate * 1/12 = **$20 accrued interest for one month.** Thus, the $40 preliminary balance in the Interest Payable account makes sense because it represents the two months' interest on the note payable that had been accrued between the last interest payment date (May 31) and the end of last month (July 31).

4-19. ***(Continued)***

Calculation for part e:

Too much was recorded as Rent Expense in August because the $510 rent payment included a prepayment of the rent for September and October. Thus, the Prepaid Rent (asset) account should be recorded for $340 (2/3 * $510), and only $170 should be included as Rent Expense in the final August income statement.

4-21. a.

Accounts Receivable

Beginning balance	$ 1,200	February collections from customers	?
February sales revenue	12,000		
Ending balance	$ 900		

Solution: $1,200 + $12,000 - ? = $900

Cash collected from customers in February = **$12,300**

Dr. Accounts Receivable	$12,000	
Cr. Sales Revenue		$12,000
Revenue from credit sales.		

Dr. Cash	$12,300	
Cr. Accounts Receivable		$12,300
Collections from customers.		

b.

Supplies on Hand

Beginning balance	$ 540	Cost of supplies used	$2,340
Cost of supplies purchased	?		
Ending balance	$ 730		

Solution: $540 + ? - $2,340 = $730

Cost of supplies purchased in February = **$2,530**

Dr. Supplies Expense	$2,340	
Cr. Supplies on Hand		$2,340
Supplies used during month.		

Dr. Supplies on Hand	$2,530	
Cr. Cash or Accounts Payable		$2,530
Supplies purchased during month.		

4-21. c.

Wages Payable

		Beginning balance	$ 410
Wages paid	$3,800	Wages accrued	4,100
		Ending balance	?

Solution: $410 + $4,100 – $3,800 = ?
Wages payable at February 28 = **$710**

Dr. Wages Payable	$3,800	
Cr. Cash		$3,800
Wages paid during month.		

Dr. Wages Expense	$4,100	
Cr. Wages Payable		$4,100
Wage expense accrued during month.		

4-23. a. Net income for October would be overstated, because an expense was not recorded.
b. Net income for November would be understated, because November expenses would include an expense from October.
c. There wouldn't be any effect on net income for the two months combined, because the overstatement and understatement offset.
d. To match revenues and expenses, which results in more accurate financial statements.

4-25. a. Commissions expense. Since DeBauge Realtors, Inc., is a service firm, the company would not report cost of goods sold, and the other costs of operating the business are likely to be less than the commissions expense that would be paid to Jeff and Kristi, and to any non-owner sales associates employed by the firm.

b. Advertising expense is material in amount. The owners of the firm would be interested in knowing how much was spent on advertising so that an assessment could be made of the relative value received (i.e., commissions revenue per dollar spent on advertising).

c. $5 Interest Expense / $50 Note Payable = **10%** effective interest rate.

d.

Operating income	$ 55,000
Interest expense	(5,000)
Earnings before taxes	$ 50,000

Average income tax rate = Income tax expense / Earnings before taxes
= $16,000 / $50,000 = **32%**

4-25. e. Since there were no changes in paid-in capital during the year, the beginning paid-in capital would also be $20,000. Thus, the beginning retained earnings would be $30,000 (total owners' equity at December 31, 1995 of $50,000 less $20,000 paid-in capital).

Retained earnings, December 31, 1995	$ 30,000
Add: Net income for the year ended December 31, 1996	34,000
Less: Dividends declared and paid in 1996	(34,000)
Retained earnings, December 31, 1996	$ 30,000

The company's dividend policy must be to distribute 100% of net income as dividends to its two stockholders. This is not uncommon for a closely-held corporation. In effect, this provides additional income to the owners besides the compensation included in the "Cost of services provided" on the income statement.

f. The corporate form of organization protects the owners by providing *limited liability*, such that their personal assets that have not been invested in the business are free from the reach of the business creditors—even in corporate bankruptcy proceedings. The primary disadvantage of the corporate form is that business *profits are taxed twice*—once at the corporate level, and a second time at the individual level when dividends are paid to stockholders. For DeBauge Realty, Inc., the *corporation* incurred $16,000 of Income Tax Expense (based on $50,000 of earnings before taxes), and Jeff and Kristi will have to pay additional *individual* income taxes on the $34,000 received as dividends (at their marginal tax rate). In the partnership form of organization, the income earned by the business passes through to the owners, and no taxes are paid by the partnership.

g. Businesses are often required to make quarterly tax payments based on their estimated annual taxable income, so DeBauge Realty, Inc., has probably already paid a substantial portion of its 1996 tax bill.

h. Working capital = Current assets – Current liabilities
Current ratio = Current assets ÷ Current liabilities

	12/31/96
Cash and short-term investments	$ 30,000
Accounts receivable, net	40,000
Total current assets (A)	$ 70,000
Accounts payable	$ 90,000
Income taxes payable	5,000
Total current liabilities (B)	$ 95,000
Working capital (A – B)	**$(25,000)**
Current ratio (A / B)	**0.74**

4-25. h. With negative working capital and a current ratio of less than 1.0, this company is experiencing a major liquidity crisis. Money will have to be borrowed on a long-term basis in order to pay current obligations unless the owners discontinue their practice of distributing 100% of net income as dividends.

i.

ROI	=	MARGIN	x	TURNOVER
NET INCOME / AVERAGE TOTAL ASSETS	=	NET INCOME / SALES *	x	SALES * / AVERAGE TOTAL ASSETS
\$34,000 / ((\$205,000 + \$195,000) / 2)	=	\$34,000 / \$142,000	x	\$142,000 / ((\$205,000 + \$195,000) / 2)
17%	=	**23.9%**	x	**0.71**

* Commissions revenue is used for sales.

ROE = Net income / Average owners' equity
= \$34,000 / ((\$50,000 + \$50,000) / 2)
= **68%**

Trend comparisons of ROI and ROE cannot be made with data for only one year. For service firms such as DeBauge Realty, Inc., ROE is more significant to analysts than ROI because the investment in assets is relatively small (as compared to that required for merchandising and manufacturing firms). Thus, the ROI measure may be distorted by the small amount of "Average total assets" in the denominator. ROE provides a better measure for closely-held service firms because the stockholders are interested in their personal return.

Chapter 5. Accounting for and Presentation of Current Assets

5-1.

Balance per bank	\$373	Balance per books	\$844
Less: Outstanding checks ($13 + $50)	(63)	Less: NSF check	(75)
		Error in recording check	
Add: Deposit in transit	450	(as \$56 instead of \$65)	(9)
Reconciled balance	\$760	Reconciled balance	\$760

5-3. a.

Dr. Accounts Receivable *(for NSF check)*	\$75	
Dr. Expense (or other account originally debited *for error*)	9	
Cr. Cash		\$84

5-3. a.

Balance Sheet						Income Statement				
Assets	=	Liabilities	+	Owners' Equity	<--	Net income	=	Revenues	–	Expenses
Accounts Receivable + 75 Cash – 84										Expense (or other account) – 9

b. The cash amount to be shown on the balance sheet is the $760 reconciled amount.

5-5. ***Solution approach:*** Set up a bank reconciliation in the usual format, enter the known information, and then work backwards to solve for the beginning balances in the company's Cash account and on the bank statement (these are referred to as the "Indicated balance" amounts in Exhibit 5-1 on page 146 in the text).

Balance per bank (i.e., Indicated balance	$?	Balance per books (i.e., Indicated balance	$?
Less: Outstanding checks	(3,000)	Less: NSF check	(400)
Add: Deposits in transit	2,100	Bank service charge	(50)
		Add: Check recording error	90
Reconciled balance	$4,800	Reconciled balance	$4,800

Key: To solve for the beginning (i.e., indicated) balances, the effects of reconciling items must be reversed out of the known ending (i.e., reconciled) balances.

a. Balance per Cash account before reconciliation = $4,800 – 90 + 400 + 50 = **$5,160**

b. Balance per bank before reconciliation = $4,800 – 2,100 + 3,000 = **$5,700**

5-7. Short-term securities that will be held until maturity (principally debt securities, like treasury bills and bank certificates of deposit) are carried at the firm's cost, which is usually approximately equal to market value because of the short duration of the investments. If the firm intends to hold certain securities (principally equity securities, like common stock) for more than a couple of months, it is appropriate to report them at market value because the unrealized gains or losses may be material in amount. Armstrong's comment that cost approximates market value communicates the fact that there isn't any significant unrealized gain (i.e., appreciation) or loss in the carrying value of the securities.

5-9.

Allowance for Bad Debts

Bad debt write-offs (from 1/1 to 11/30)	?	1/1/96 balance	$13,400
		Bad debt expense (from 1/1 to 11/30)	21,462
		11/30/96 balance	9,763
Adjustment required	?		
		12/31/96 balance	$ 9,500

a. ***Solution approach*:** The bad debt write-offs from January through November can be determined by subtracting the November 30 balance from the total of the beginning balance and the bad debts expense recognized for the first 11 months.
Bad debt write-offs = $13,400 + $21,462 – $9,763 = **$25,099**

b. The adjustment required at December 31, 1996 can be determined by comparing the November 30 balance in the allowance account to the desired ending balance.
Bad debt expense adjustment = $9,763 – $9,500 = **$263**

	Dr.	Cr.
Dr. Allowance for Bad Debts	$263	
Cr. Bad Debts Expense		$263

To adjust the allowance account to the appropriate balance, and to correct the overstatement of expense recorded in the January through November period.

Balance Sheet				Income Statement		
Assets =	Liabilities +	Owners' Equity <--	Net income =	Revenues –		Expenses
Allowance for Bad Debts + 263	*(Note: A reduction in an expense increases net income, and a reduction in a contra-asset account increases total assets.)*					Bad Debts Expense + 263

c. The write-off will not have any effect on 1996 net income, because the write-off decreases both the accounts receivable asset and the allowance account contra-asset for equal amounts. Net income was affected when the expense was recognized. These relationships are discussed and illustrated on pages 151-152 in the text.

5-11. a.

Allowance for Bad Debts

Bad debt write-offs (during the year)........	$11,800	12/31/95 balance	$17,900
		Bad debt expense	?
		12/31/96 balance	$ 9,500

Bad debt expense = $11,800 – $17,900 + $9,500 = **$3,400**

5-11. b. 1. Working capital would not be affected because the write-off entry decreases both the accounts receivable asset and the allowance account contra-asset by equal amounts.

Dr. Allowance for Bad Debts	$3,100	
Cr. Accounts Receivable		$3,100

To write off a past due account as uncollectible.

Balance Sheet			Income Statement		
Assets	= Liabilities	+ Owners' Equity <--	Net income	= Revenues	− Expenses
Accounts Receivable − 3,100 Allowance for Bad Debts + 3,100					

2. Net income would not be affected by the write-off entry because it does not adjust any expense or revenue accounts. ROI would not be affected because net income and total assets are not changed.

c. Sales were *probably* lower in 1996 because the accounts receivable balance has decreased during the year—but this cannot be determined for sure without information about the cash collections of accounts receivable.

5-13. ***Solution approach:*** Net realizable value = Accounts receivable − Allowance for bad debts. The balance sheet presentation of this information at December 31, 1996 (ending balances) is provided with the problem information. Your task is to work backwards to determine the balances in these accounts at December 31, 1995 (beginning balances).

Accounts Receivable

12/31/95 balance.	$?	Cash collections from customers	$410,000
Sales on account.	400,000		
12/31/96 balance.	$ 50,000		

December 31, 1995 balance = $410,000 − $400,000 + $50,000 = **$60,000.** This makes sense because Carr Co. collected more accounts during the year than it created in new accounts with credit sales.

5-13. ***(Continued)*** **Allowance for Bad Debts**

Debit		Credit	
Bad debt write-offs (during the year).	$15,000	12/31/95 balance	$?
		Bad debt expense	12,000
		12/31/96 balance	$ 7,000

December 31, 1995 balance = $7,000 + $15,000 – $12,000 = **$10,000.** This makes sense because Carr Co. wrote-off more accounts during the year than it added to the allowance account with the bad debts expense adjustment.

At December 31, 1995:

Accounts receivable	$60,000	
Less: Allowance for bad debts	(10,000)	$50,000

5-15. Selection and training relate to the efficiency with which a firm's operations are carried out. Also, having qualified and trained personnel should result in more accuracy of the firm's record-keeping than having unqualified, untrained personnel.

5-17. a. 2% * $340,000,000 * 90% = **$6,120,000,** or $6.12 million.

b. Sales during last 10 days of the year = ($340,000,000 / 365) average day's sales *10 days = $9,315,000. Discount expected = 2% * $9,315,000 * 90%= **$167,670.** This should be the balance in the allowance for cash discounts.

c. By paying within 10 days instead of 30 days, the customers are "investing" funds for 20 days, and receiving slightly more than a 2 percent return on their investment (for a $100 obligation, the return is $2 on an investment of $98). But ROI is expressed as an annual percentage rate, and there are slightly more than 18 twenty-day periods in a year. Thus the annual ROI is a little greater than 36 percent. *(See Business Procedure Capsule 9 on page 153 in the text.)*

5-19. a.

4½ months		5½ months	
6/15 date of note	10/31 year end		4/15 maturity date

Interest earned = $4,500 principal * 13.8% rate * 4½/12 time = **$232.88**

Dr. Interest Receivable	$232.88	
Cr. Interest Revenue		$232.88

To accrue interest earned on a short-term note.

5-19. a.

Balance Sheet				Income Statement		
Assets	= Liabilities	+ Owners' Equity	<-- Net income	= Revenues	- Expenses
Interest Receivable + 232.88				Interest Revenue + 232.88	

b. ***Solution approach*:** What accounts are affected, and how are they affected? Cash is being received for note principal and 10 month's interest. Notes receivable is reduced because the note is being paid off. Interest receivable accrued at 10/31 is being collected. Interest revenue for 5½ months from 10/31 to 4/15 has been earned.

	Dr.	Cr.
Dr. Cash ($4,500 + ($4,500 * 13.8% * 10/12))	$5,017.50	
Cr. Note Receivable		$4,500.00
Cr. Interest Receivable (accrued at 10/31)		232.88
Cr. Interest Revenue ($4,500 * 13.8% * 5½/12)		284.62

To record the collection of principal and interest at the maturity date of a short-term note (for which some interest had been previously accrued).

Balance Sheet				Income Statement	
Assets	= Liabilities	+ Owners' Equity	<-- Net income	= Revenues	- Expenses
Cash + 5,017.50				Interest Revenue + 284.62	
Note Receivable - 4,500					
Interest Receivable - 232.88					

5-21. a. ***Ending inventory calculations:***

	FIFO	LIFO
Blowers	10 of 11/7 @ 200 = $2,000	10 of 1/21 @ 200 = $2,000
Mowers	20 of 9/20 @ 210 = $4,200	20 of 4/6 @ 210 = $4,200
	5 of 8/15 @ 215 = 1,075	5 of 5/22 @ 215 = 1,075
	$5,275	$5,275

***Analysis of results*:** In this problem, there is no difference between ending inventories, and therefore there won't be any difference between cost of goods sold under either alternative. Neither the amount of goods available for sale (the sum of the beginning inventory and

5-21. a. purchases amounts) nor the amount of ending inventory are affected by the inventory cost flow assumption used. Why? Look carefully at the cost per unit of inventory items that were purchased during the year. Notice that the costs per unit of the beginning inventory and the cost per unit of items purchased on September 20 and November 7 are the same.

b. Probably LIFO, because the higher cost of the most recent (last-in) purchase will become part of the cost of goods sold, thus increasing cost, decreasing profits, and decreasing the firm's income tax obligation.

5-23. ***Solution approach*:** Calculate goods available for sale in units and dollars, and ending inventory in units. These amounts are the same for both FIFO and LIFO under either a periodic or a perpetual inventory system.

	Units @ Cost	Amount
Beginning inventory	150 @ $30 =	$ 4,500
Purchases	70 @ 33 =	2,310
	90 @ 35 =	3,150
	140 @ 36 =	5,040
	50 @ 38 =	1,900
Goods available for sale	500	$16,900
Sales	(300)	=======
Ending inventory	200 units	
	===	

		Units @ Cost	Amount	Total
a. FIFO periodic cost of goods sold		150 @ $30 =	$4,500	
		70 @ 33 =	2,310	
		80 @ 35 =	2,800	$ 9,610
FIFO periodic ending inventory		10 @ 35 =	350	
		140 @ 36 =	5,040	
		50 @ 38 =	1,900	7,290
				$16,900
				=======
LIFO periodic cost of goods sold		50 @ $38 =	$1,900	
		140 @ 36 =	5,040	
		90 @ 35 =	3,150	
		20 @ 33 =	660	$10,750
LIFO periodic ending inventory		150 @ 30 =	$4,500	
		50 @ 33 =	1,650	6,150
				$16,900
				=======
b. FIFO perpetual cost of goods sold	3/7 sale	100 @ $30 =	$3,000	
	9/28 sale	50 @ 30 =	1,500	
		50 @ 33 =	1,650	
	12/4 sale	20 @ 33 =	660	
		80 @ 35 =	2,800	$ 9,610
FIFO perpetual ending inventory . .		10 @ 35 =	350	
		140 @ 36 =	5,040	
		50 @ 38 =	1,900	7,290
				$16,900
				=======

5-23. b. ***(Continued)***

LIFO perpetual cost of goods sold	3/7 sale	70 @ $33 =	$2,310	
		30 @ 30 =	900	
	9/28 sale	100 @ 36 =	3,600	
	12/4 sale	50 @ 38 =	1,900	
		40 @ 36 =	1,440	
		10 @ 35 =	350	$10,500
LIFO perpetual ending inventory		120 @ 30 =	$3,600	
		80 @ 35 =	2,800	6,400
				$16,900
				=======

c. Under FIFO, the periodic and perpetual inventory systems *always* result in the same dollar amounts being assigned to ending inventory and cost of goods sold—once first-in, always first-in—and the timing of the application of the FIFO rules makes no difference. Under LIFO, the "last-in cost" changes each time another inventory item is purchased. Thus, the timing of the application of the LIFO rules is relevant, and different results will occur under the periodic and perpetual systems. These relationships are discussed in Business Procedure Capsule 10 on pages 167-168 in the text.

5-25. The older, relatively lower costs are going out to cost of goods sold as inventory levels are reduced (or liquidated). Revenues reflect current price levels. Thus, inventory reductions result in profit increases under LIFO, because older, lower costs are being subtracted from current selling prices. Inventory reductions of FIFO firms may also cause profit increases, because the cost of inventory reductions may also be less than current cost, but the profit effect will not be as great as for a firm that uses LIFO. This situation is often referred to as a *LIFO liquidation.* You may find it helpful to review the discussion of this issue on pages 163 (bottom) through 166 (top) in the text.

5-27. ROI = Net income / Average assets

		FIFO	*LIFO*
a.	Net income	$120	$100
	/ Average assets	600	580
	= ROI	**20%**	**17.2%**

***Analysis of results*:** When prices are *rising,* LIFO results in a higher cost of goods sold amount and a lower ending inventory amount, as compared to FIFO. Thus, net income is lower, assets are lower, and ROI is lower under LIFO.

		FIFO	*LIFO*
b.	Net income	$130	$140
	/ Average assets	650	620
	= ROI	**20%**	**22.6%**

5-27. b. ***Analysis of results*:** When prices are *falling,* all of the above effects (from part *a*) are reversed. LIFO may result in a lower cost of goods sold amount in any given year (since the most recent, lowest costs, are treated as cost of goods sold). If a liquidation occurs, the ending inventory amount will also be lowered in that year, as compared to FIFO. Thus, net income will be higher under LIFO, and ROI will also be higher, as compared to FIFO.

5-29. a. *March 1*

	Dr.	Cr.
Dr. Prepaid Insurance	$3,000	
Cr. Cash		$3,000

To record the payment of a one-year insurance premium.

Balance Sheet					Income Statement				
Assets	=	Liabilities	+	Owners' Equity <--	Net income	=	Revenues	-	Expenses
Prepaid Insurance + 3,000 Cash - 3,000									

b. *Each month-end*:

	Dr.	Cr.
Dr. Insurance Expense	$250	
Cr. Prepaid Insurance		$250

To record the expiration of prepaid insurance each month.

Balance Sheet					Income Statement				
Assets	=	Liabilities	+	Owners' Equity <--	Net income	=	Revenues	-	Expenses
Prepaid Insurance - 250									Insurance Exp. - 250

c. At August 31, 6 months of insurance coverage has been used, and 6 months is still to be used. So one-half of the original premium of $3,000, or $1,500 is prepaid and will be shown on the August 31 balance sheet as a current asset.

d. The prepaid amount is $4,500, for coverage for the 18 months. Only $3,000 of this amount is a current asset, because of the one-year time frame for current assets. Thus, $1,500 of the prepaid amount is technically a noncurrent asset.

e. To result in better matching of revenues and expenses, and a more meaningful net income amount. Although the expenditure of cash has been made, the item relates to the earning of revenue in a subsequent accounting period.

5-31.

	Current Assets	***Current Liabilities***	***Owners' Equity***	***Net Income***
b. Determined that the Allowance for Bad Debts balance should be increased by $2,200.	Allowance for Bad Debts – 2,200			Bad Debts Expense – 2,200
c. Recognized bank service $30 for the month.	Cash – 30			Service Charge Exp. – 30
d. Received $25 cash for interest receivable that had been accrued in a prior month.	Cash + 25 Interest Receivable – 25			
e. Purchased five units of a new item of inventory on account at a cost of $35 each.	Inventory + 175	Accounts Payable + 175		
f. Purchased 10 more units of the above item at a cost of $38 each.	Inventory + 380	Accounts Payable + 380		
g. Sold eight of the items purchased (in *e* and *f* above), and recognized the cost of goods sold using the FIFO cost-flow assumption.	Inventory – 289 *(5 units @ $35, 3 units @ $38)*			Cost of Goods Sold – 289

5-33.

	Current Assets	***Current Liabilities***	***Owners' Equity***	***Net Income***
b. Recorded estimated bad debts in the amount of $700.	Allowance for Bad Debts – 700			Bad Debts Expense – 700
c. Wrote off an overdue account receivable of $520.	Accounts Receivable – 520 Allowance for Doubtful Accounts + 520		*(Net realizable value of accounts receivable is not affected.)*	

5-33.

	Current Assets	*Current Liabilities*	*Owners' Equity*	*Net Income*
d. Converted a customer's $1,200 overdue account receivable into a note.	Notes Receivable + 1,200 Accounts Receivable - 1,200			
e. Accrued $48 of interest earned on the note (in *d* above).	Interest Receivable + 48			Interest Revenue + 48
f. Collected the accrued interest (in *e* above).	Cash + 48 Interest Rec. - 48			
g. Recorded $4,000 of sales, 80% of which were on account.	Cash + 800 Accounts Rec. + 3,200			Sales + 4,000
h. Recognized cost of goods sold in the amount of $3,200.	Inventory - 3,200			Cost of Goods Sold - 3,200
i. Recorded estimated cash discounts for 2% of credit sales (in *g* above).	Allowance for Cash Discounts - 64			Cash Discounts on Sales - 64

Chapter 6. Accounting for and Presentation of Property, Plant, and Equipment, and Other Noncurrent Assets

6-1. a. Allocate the purchase cost in proportion to appraised values.
Cost of land = ($20,000 / ($80,000 + $20,000)) * $90,000 = **$18,000**

b. Land is not a depreciable asset. Management would want as much of the purchase price as feasible to be assigned to assets whose cost will become a tax-deductible expense in future years—reducing taxable income and income taxes payable.

6-1. c. All ordinary and necessary costs incurred by Dorsey Co. in order to get the land ready for its intended use should be added to the Land account. Thus, the cost included in the Land account is the total amount paid, plus the cost of razing building. Note that no costs are added to Dorsey Co.'s Buildings account because the building was not acquired with the intent to be used as a building.

Cost of land = $90,000 + $10,000 = **$100,000**

d. Appriased values are be used because they represent the *current* asset values (at the time of purchase by Dorsey Co.). The old original cost data represent what the relative asset values were (at the time of purchase by Bibb Co.), which is not relevant to Dorsey Co.

6-3. a. Expense. Routine repair and maintenance costs would not increase the useful life or estimated salvage of the vehicles, so the "economic benefits" of these expenditures relate only to the current year.

b. Asset. The cost of developing the coal mine should be capitalized (as a natural resource) because the extraction of coal will generate revenues in future years. The $60,000 cost of developing the coal mine will be recorded as depletion expense (at a rate of six cents per ton extracted).

c. Asset. This cost should be added to the Building account because it will extend the useful life of the asset.

d. Expense. Advertising costs are *always* treated as expenses in the year incurred because it is impossible to determine to what extent, if any, future-period revenues will be affected by current-period advertising expenditures.

e. Asset. This cost should be added to the Land account because it is an ordinary and necessary cost incurred to get the land ready for its intended use.

6-5. a. Repair cost capitalized in error = $20,000.

Depreciation expense in current year on above amount:

To be depreciated	$20,000
Remaining life	5 years
Depreciation expense in current year	$ 4,000

To correct the error:

Operating income originally reported	$160,000
Increase in repair expense	(20,000)
Decrease in depreciation expense	4,000
Corrected operating income	**$144,000**

6-5. b. ***ROI for current year based on original data:***
ROI = Operating income / Average total assets
= $160,000 / (($940,000 + $1,020,000) / 2 = **16.3%**

ROI for current year based on corrected data:

Year-end assets originally reported		$1,020,000
Less net book value of mistakenly capitalized repair expense:		
Cost	$20,000	
Less accumulated depreciation	(4,000)	(16,000)
Corrected year-end assets		$1,004,000

ROI = Operating income / Average total assets
= $144,000 / (($940,000 + $1,004,000) / 2) = **14.8%**

c. In subsequent years, depreciation expense will be too high, net income will be too low, and average assets will be too high. Thus, ROI will be too low.

6-7. a. Amount to be depreciated = Cost – Salvage value
Annual depreciation expense = Amount to be depreciated / Useful life
Annual depreciation expense = ($80,000 – $8,000) / 8 = $9,000 per year
After 5 years, accumulated depreciation = $9,000 * 5 = **$45,000**

b. Straight-line rate = 1 / 8 = 12.5%. Double-declining rate = 12.5% * 2 = **25%**

			At End of Year	
Year	*Net Book Value at Beginning of Year*	*Depreciation Expense*	*Accumulated Depreciation*	*Net Book Value*
1	$80,000	$80,000 * 25% = $20,000	$20,000	$60,000
2	60,000	60,000 * 25% = 15,000	35,000	45,000
3	45,000	45,000 * 25% = **11,250**	46,250	33,750

c. Sum of the digits for an 8-year life = 8 + 7 + 6 + 5 + 4 + 3 + 2 + 1 = 36 digits
Amount to be depreciated = $80,000 cost – $8,000 salvage value = $72,000

Solution approach: Accumulated depreciation at the end of the fifth year equals the sum of the depreciation expense amounts recorded in the first five years.
After 5 years, accumulated depreciation = ((8 + 7 + 6 + 5 + 4) / 36) * $72,000
= (30 / 36) * $72,000 = **$60,000**

6-7. c. ***(Continued)***

Under sum-of-the-years'-digits, accumulated depreciation after 5 years is $15,000 higher ($60,000 – $45,000), than under straight-line because of the accelerated depreciation pattern.

d. **Net book value = Cost – Accumulated depreciation. After 8 years, the asset will have been fully depreciated to its estimated salvage value of $8,000 under each method. Accumulated depreciation will be $72,000, and net book value will be $8,000 ($80,000 – $72,000).**

6-9.

Estimated useful life	7 years
Cost of machine	$9,600
Estimated salvage value	(1,200)
Amount to be depreciated	$8,400

1. ***Straight-line depreciation*:**
Annual depreciation expense = $8,400 / 7 years = **$1,200 per year**
Depreciation expense for 1996 (9 months) = $1,200 * 9/12 = **$900**
Depreciation expense for 1997 (12 months) = **$1,200**

2. ***Sum-of-the-years' digits depreciation:***
Sum of the digits for a 7-year life = (7 + 6 + 5 + 4 +3 +2 + 1) = 28 digits
Depreciation expense of first year of asset's life = 7/28 * $8,400 = $2,100
Depreciation expense of second year of asset's life = 6/28 * $8,400 = $1,800
Depreciation expense for 1996 = 9 months of the first year's expense
= $2,100 * 9/12 = **$1,575**
Depreciation expense for 1997 = (3 months of the first year's expense + 9 months of the second year's expense)
= (3/12 * $2,100) + (9/12 * $1,800)
= $525 + $1,350 = **$1,875**

6-11.

Estimated useful life	4 years
Cost of machine	$120,000
Estimated salvage value	(20,000)
Amount to be depreciated	$100,000

a.

Year	*Net Book Value at Beginning of Year*	*Net Book Value at End of Year*	*Depreciation Expense*	*Accumulated Depreciation*
1996	$120,000	$80,000	**$40,000**	$ 40,000
1997	80,000	50,000	**30,000**	70,000
1998	50,000	30,000	**20,000**	90,000
1999	30,000	20,000	**10,000**	100,000

6-11. a. ***(Continued)***

The **sum-of-the-years'-digits method** is being used because the depreciation expense recorded each year is decreasing at a constant rate representing the 4/10, 3/10, 2/10, 1/10 pattern * $100,000.

b.

Year	*Net Book Value at Beginning of Year*	*Net Book Value at End of Year*	*Depreciation Expense*	*Accumulated Depreciation*
1996	$120,000	$98,000	**$22,000**	$ 22,000
1997	98,000	66,000	**32,000**	54,000
1998	66,000	38,000	**28,000**	82,000
1999	38,000	20,000	**18,000**	100,000

The **units of production method** is being used. At first glance, no clear pattern can be seen in the amount of depreciation expense recorded each year. However, based on the machine's productive capacity of 50,000 units and the actual production data provided for 1996-1999, the depreciation expense amounts shown above can be easily verified.

c.

Year	*Net Book Value at Beginning of Year*	*Net Book Value at End of Year*	*Depreciation Expense*	*Accumulated Depreciation*
1996	$120,000	$60,000	**$60,000**	$ 60,000
1997	60,000	30,000	**30,000**	90,000
1998	30,000	20,000	**10,000**	100,000
1999	20,000	20,000	**0**	100,000

The **double-declining balance (200%) method** is being used. Notice that the expense pattern is extremely accelerated in this case. Using the double-declining balance method for an asset with a 4-year useful life results in an annual depreciation rate of 50% (25% straight-line rate * 2) of the asset's net book value. In 1998, the machine became fully depreciated after only $10,000 was recorded as depreciation expense, even though the calculated amount was higher (50% * $30,000 = $15,000).

d.

Year	*Net Book Value at Beginning of Year*	*Net Book Value at End of Year*	*Depreciation Expense*	*Accumulated Depreciation*
1996	$120,000	$95,000	**$25,000**	$ 25,000
1997	95,000	70,000	**25,000**	50,000
1998	70,000	45,000	**25,000**	75,000
1999	45,000	20,000	**25,000**	100,000

The **straight-line method** is being used because an equal amount of depreciation expense is recorded each year, which represents 1/4 * $100,000.

6-13. a. Estimated useful life .... 5 years
Cost of machine $210,000
Estimated salvage value .... (20,000)
Amount to be depreciated $190,000

Straight-line depreciation:
Annual depreciation expense = $190,000 / 5 = **$38,000 per year**
Depreciation expense for 1998 = **$38,000**
Accumulated depreciation at December 31, 1998 = $38,000 * 2½ years = **$95,000**

b. ***Double-declining balance method:***
Straight-line rate = 1 / 5 = 20%. Double-declining rate = 20% * 2 = **40%**

				At End of Year	
Year	*Net Book Value at Beginning of Year#*	*Depreciation Expense*		*Accumulated Depreciation*	*Net Book Value*
1996	$210,000	$210,000 * 40% * ½ =	$42,000	$ 42,000	$168,000
1997	168,000	168,000 * 40% =	67,200	109,200	100,800
1998	100,800	100,800 * 40% =	**40,320**	149,520	**60,480**

July 1 for 1996, and January 1 for 1997 and 1998.

6-15. Straight-line depreciation is used for financial reporting purposes because depreciation expense will be lower than under an accelerated depreciation method. Accelerated depreciation is used for tax purposes so taxes will be minimized.

6-17. Alpha, Inc. should have a higher ROI than Beta Co. Alpha, Inc.'s plant is older and will be depreciated to a greater extent than Beta Co.'s. Thus, Alpha, Inc.'s asset base will be lower, so its ROI will be higher. The implication for Beta Co. is that because of its lower ROI, its ability to raise capital will be reduced unless it has production and/or technological advantages or efficiencies.

6-19. a. Depreciation expense for 1996 is the *increase* in the amount of accumulated depreciation from the beginning balance sheet to the ending balance sheet, or $18,000 ($42,000 – $24,000).

b. 1. The cost of the asset is the net book value plus the accumulated depreciation, or $28,000 + $42,000 = **$70,000.**

2. It is difficult to determine which depreciation *method* is being used because the acquisition date of the asset is not known. However, the *amount* to be depreciated can be determined, as follows:

6-19. b. 2. ***(Continued)***

Estimated useful life	4 years
Cost of machine	$70,000
Estimated salvage value	(10,000)
Amount to be depreciated	$60,000

The straight-line method is not being used because the annual depreciation expense would be $15,000 ($60,000 / 4 years), and not $18,000 as determined in part *a*. The **sum-of the-years'-digits method** is being used because the balance of the accumulated depreciation account has increased from $24,000 to $42,000, which is consistent with the depreciation pattern under this method. For an asset with a 4-year useful life, the depreciation pattern would be: 4/10, 3/10, 2/10, 1/10.

		At End of Year	
Year	*Depreciation Expense*	*Accumulated Depreciation*	*Net Book Value*
1	4/10 * $60,000 = **$24,000**	**$24,000**	**$46,000**
2	3/10 * 60,000 = **18,000**	**42,000**	**28,000**
3	2/10 * 60,000 = 12,000	54,000	16,000
4	1/10 * 60,000 = 6,000	60,000	10,000

3. At December 31, 1996, the accumulated depreciation of $42,000 represents 2 years of depreciation expense, so the acquisition date of the machine must have been on or near **January 1, 1995.**

c.

Dr. Cash	$23,600	
Dr. Accumulated depreciation	42,000	
Dr. Loss on sale of machine	4,400	
Cr. Machine		$70,000

To record the sale of a machine at a loss.

Balance Sheet				Income Statement		
Assets	= Liabilities	+ Owners' Equity	<-- Net income	= Revenues	− Expenses	
Cash +23,600 Machine −70,000 Accumulated Depreciation +42,000	*(A decrease in a contra-asset account increases assets).*				Loss on Sale of Machine −4,400	

6-21. a.

List price of new computer	$110,000
Less: Trade-in allowance	(12,000)
Cash to be paid	$ 98,000

$21,000 net book value = ($85,000 cost – accumulated depreciation)
Accumulated depreciation = $64,000

Cost of new asset in trade-in transaction:

Net book value of old asset	$ 21,000
Cash paid "to boot"	98,000
Cost of new computer	$119,000

b.

Dr. Computer equipment (cost of new)	$119,000	
Dr. Accumulated depreciation (on old)	64,000	
Cr. Cash		$98,000
Cr. Computer Equipment (cost of old)		85,000

To record the trade-in of an old computer for a new computer.

Balance Sheet			Income Statement		
Assets =	Liabilities +	Owners' Equity <--	Net income =	Revenues –	Expenses
Computer Equipment (cost of old) –85,000 Accumuated Depreciation (on old) +64,000 Cash –98,000 Computer Equipment (cost of new) +119,000			*(Note that the trade-in transaction effects* ***assets only,*** *and has no effect on the income statement because the earnings process of the old asset will continue with the use of the new asset.)*		

6-23. a.

List price of new machine	$40,000
Less: Trade-in allowance	(3,600)
Cash to be paid	$36,400

Cost of new asset in trade-in transaction:

Cost of old asset	$25,000
Accumulated depreciation on old asset	(18,000)
Current year's depreciation on old asset	(2,000)

6-23. a. ***(Continued)***

Net book value of old asset	$ 5,000
Cash paid "to boot"	36,400
Cost of new machine	**$41,400**

b.

Dr. Machine (cost of new)	$41,400	
Dr. Accumulated Depreciation (on old)	18,000	
Dr. Depreciation Expense (for current year on old) #	2,000	
Cr. Cash		$36,400
Cr. Machine (cost of old)		25,000

To record the current year's depreciation expense, and the trade-in of an old machine for a new machine.

A common bookkeeping practice is to record the entry for the current year's depreciation expense on the old asset *first,* and then record the trade-in (or sale) transaction separately. This approach brings the accumulated depreciation account up-to-date, which then makes it easier to determine what the net book value of the old asset was at the time it was traded in (or sold). The results are the same either way:

Dr. Depreciation Expense (for current year on old)	$2,000	
Cr. Accumulated Depreciation (on old)		$2,000

Dr. Machine (cost of new)	$41,400	
Dr. Accumulated Depreciation (on old)	20,000	
Cr. Cash		$36,400
Cr. Machine (cost of old)		25,000

Balance Sheet		Income Statement
Assets = Liabilities + Owners' Equity <--		Net income = Revenues - Expenses
Machine (cost of old) - 25,000 Accumulated Depreciation (old) + 18,000 Cash - 36,400 Machine (cost of new) + 41,400	*(Note that the trade-in transaction effects assets only, and has no effect on the income statement because the earnings process of the old asset will continue with the use of the new asset. As explained above, the depreciation expense entry is really a separate transaction from the trade-in.*	Depreciation Expense - 2,000

c. Installation costs for a machine that will be used in the firm's operations are ordinary and necessary costs incurred to get the machine ready for its intended purpose. Thus, the $700 should be capitalized (i.e., added to the Machine account).

6-25. a. If *any* of the four criteria (listed on page 206 in the text) for capitalizing a lease are met, the lease should be accounted for as a capital lease rather than an operating lease.

1. **Maybe.** The problem does not state that *ownership* of the computer system is transferred to Carey, Inc. during the term of the lease, but it does state that the system was *aquired.* Thus, its not clear whether title to the asset transferred.
2. **Yes.** The option to purchase the computer system for $1 at the end of four years is a "bargain purchase option."
3. **Yes.** The 75% test is met because the lease term of 4 years is 100% of the economic life of the computer system.
4. **Yes.** The 90% test is met because the present value of the lease payments is $10,197.95which is 100% (rounded) of the $10,200 fair value of the asset.

b.

Annual lease payments (paid at the end of each year)	$ 3,500
Present value factor (Table 6-3, 4 periods, 14% discount rate)	* 2.9137
Present value of lease payments (amount to be capitalized)	**$10,197.95**

Dr. Equipment	$10,200	
Cr. Capital Lease Liability		$10,200

To record a capital lease transaction at the present value of future lease payments (amount rounded to the nearest $10).

Balance Sheet			Income Statement	
Assets =	Liabilities +	Owners' Equity <--	Net income =	Revenues - Expenses
Equipment + 10,200	Capital Lease Liability + 10,200			

c.

Annual lease payment		$ 3,500
Beginning balance, capital lease liability	$10,200	
Interest rate	* 14%	
Interest expense (for first year of lease term)		(1,428)
Payment of principal (reduction of capital lease liability)		**$2,072**

Dr. Interest Expense	$1,428	
Dr. Capital Lease Liability	2,072	
Cr. Cash		$3,500

To record the first annual lease payment on a capital lease.

6-25. c. ***(Continued)***

Balance Sheet				Income Statement		
Assets	= Liabilities	+ Owners' Equity	<-- Net income	= Revenues	–	Expenses
Cash – 3,500	Capital Lease Liability – 2,072					Interest Expense – 1,428

d. **In addition to the $1,428 of Interest Expense** on the capital lease liability, **Deprecitaion Expense of $2,550** ($10,200 / 4 years) on the equipment should also be recognized in the income statement. Note that the amount of interest expense will *decrease* each year of the lease term because the capital lease liability is reduced each time an annual lease payment is made.

e. As discussed and illustrated in the text on pages 214-215, the *economic effect* of a long-term capital lease is not any different than the purchase of an asset with borrowed funds. In substance, the firm has acquired virtually all of the rights and benefits of ownership—so the accounting for a capital lease should be consistent with that of an asset purchase.

6-27.

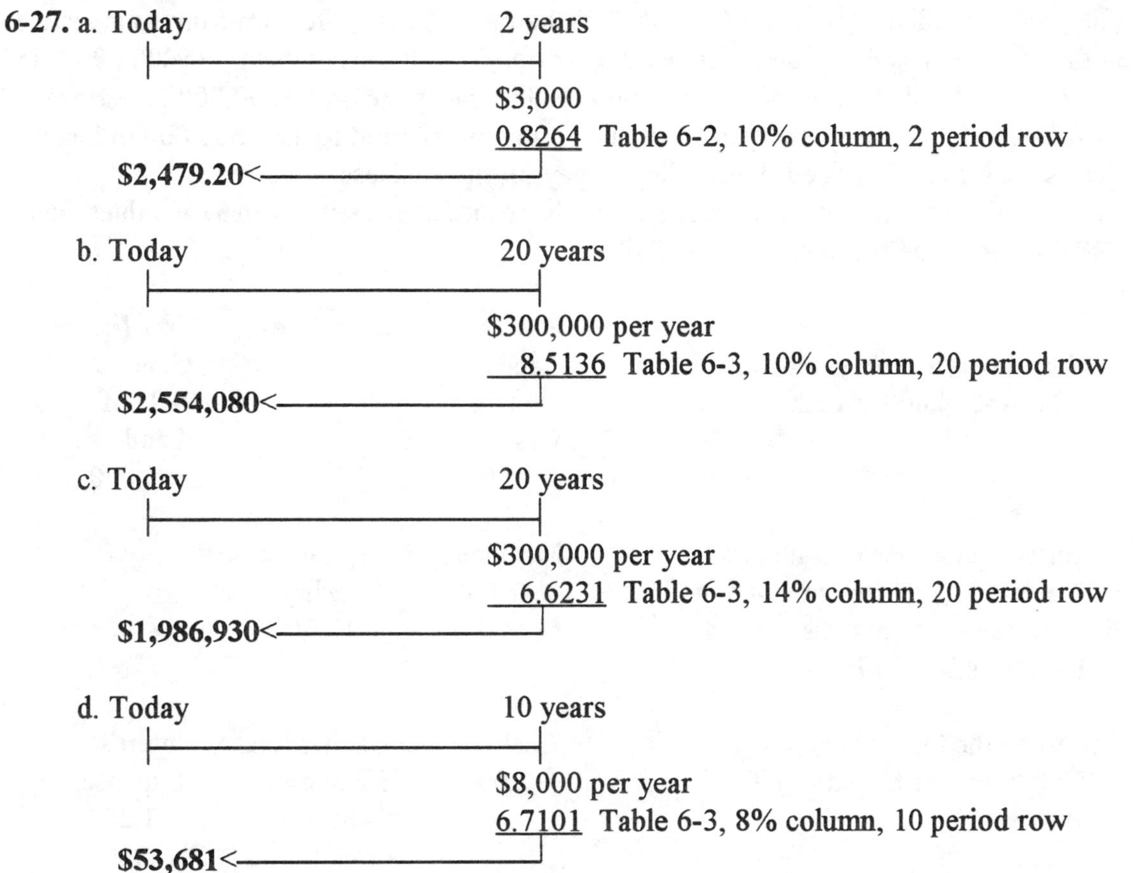

6-29. The present value factor for a single amount for 5 periods, at a discount rate of 16% in Table 6-2 is 0.4761. Thus, $100,000 * 0.4761 = **$47,610** present value.

a. Since interest will be compounded twice per year, the number of periods is 10 (5 years * 2) and the rate is 8% (16% / 2). The present factor for 10 periods at 8% from Table 6-2 is 0.4632. Thus, $100,000 * 0.4632 = **$46,320** present value.

b. The number of periods now becomes 20 (5 years * 4 quarters per year), and the rate becomes 4% (16% / 4 quarters per year). The present value factor for 20 periods at 4% from Table 6-2 is 0.4564. Thus, $100,000 * 0.4564 = **$45,640** present value.

c. The present value factor at 12% for 5 periods in Table 6-2 is 0.5674. Thus, $100,000 * 0.5674 = **$56,740** present value.

d. The present value factor at 20% for 5 periods in Table 6-2 is 0.4019. Thus, $100,000 * 0.4019 = **$40,190** present value.

e. The present value factor at 16% for 3 periods in Table 6-2 is 0.6407. Thus, $100,000 * 0.6407 = **$64,070** present value.

f. The present value factor at 16% for 7 periods in Table 6-2 is 0.3538. Thus, $100,000 * 0.3538 = **$35,380** present value.

6-31. a. Yes, because of the above-average ROI of 18%, I could afford to invest **$40,000** more than $200,000 and still earn a 15% ROI—which is the rate I'd expect to earn from an investment in this type of business. The excess earnings offered by this investment = ($200,000 * 18%) - ($200,000 * 15%) = $36,000 – $30,000 = **$6,000 per year** on a $200,000 investment. At an ROI of 15%, an investment of **$240,000** would be required to earn $36,000 of income, so that is the maximum price I'd be willing to pay for the business.

b. Each of the individual assets acquired would be recorded at their fair market values, and $40,000 would be recorded as "Goodwill."

6-33.

	Assets	***Liabilities***	***Net Income***
b. Sold land that had originally cost $9,000 for $14,000 in cash.	Land - 9,000 Cash + 14,000		Gain on Sale of Land + 5,000
c. Acquired a new machine under a capital lease. The present value of future lease payments, discounted at 10%, was $12,000.	Machine + 12,000	Capital Lease Liability + 12,000	
d. Recorded the first annual payment of $2,000 for the leased machine (in *c* above).	Cash - 2,000	Capital Lease Liability - 800	Interest Expense - 1,200

*(Interest = $12,000 * 10%).*

6-33. ***(Continued)***	***Assets***	***Liabilities***	***Net Income***
e. Recorded a $6,000 payment for the cost of developing and registering a trademark.	Trademark + 6,000 Cash - 6,000		
f. Recognized the periodic amortization on the trademark (in *e* above) using a 40-year useful life.	Trademark - 150		Amortization Expense - 150
g. Sold used production equipment for $16,000 in cash. The equipment originally cost $40,000. The accumulated depreciation account had a balance of $22,000 before adjusting for a $1,000 year-to-date depreciation entry that must be recorded before the sale of the equipment is recorded.	Accumulated Depreciation - 1,000, + 23,000 Equipment - 40,000 Cash + 16,000		Depreciation Expense - 1,000 Loss on Sale of Equipment - 1,000
h. Traded in an old tractor plus $12,000 for a new tractor having a $20,000 list price. The old tractor had cost $16,000 and had a net book value of $7,000 at the time of the exchange. A trade-in allowance of $8,000 was given for the old tractor.	Tractor (old) - 16,000 Cash - 12,000 Accumulated Depreciation (old) + 9,000 Tractor (new) + 19,000	*(Note: No gain or loss is recorded on the trade-in.)*	

Cost of new asset in trade-in transaction:

Net book value of old asset	$ 7,000
Cash paid "to boot"	12,000
Cost of new tractor	**$19,000**

Chapter 7. Accounting for and Presentation of Liabilities

7-1. a. Discount basis means interest is paid in advance.
Proceeds = Face amount of note – Interest
= $300,000 – ($300,000 * 9% * 6/12)
= $300,000 – $13,500 = **$286,500**

7-1. a. ***(Continued)***

April 15, 1996

Dr. Cash	$286,500	
Dr. Discount on Notes Payable	13,500	
Cr. Notes Payable		$300,000

To record the proceeds of a short-term note payable (discount basis).

Balance Sheet			Income Statement		
Assets	= Liabilities	+ Owners' Equity <--	Net income	= Revenues	– Expenses
Cash + 286,500	Notes Payable + 300,000 Discount on Notes Payable - 13,500				

(Note: The discount account is a contra liability, so the initial carrying value of the note is equal to the cash proceeds received—which is the approach taken when interest is calculated on a straight basis.)

b. The note was dated April 15, 1996, so 2½ months have passed from the time the note was signed until the June 30, 1996 fiscal year-end. Interest = $300,000 * 9% * 2½/12 = **$5,625**

c. Current liability = Face amount less discount balance.
= $300,000 – ($13,500 – $5,625)
= $300,000 – $7,875 = **$292,125**

7-3. a. *3/31/96*

Dr. Payroll Tax Expense	$4,800	
Cr. Payroll Taxes Payable		$4,800

To accrue payroll taxes for the year.

Balance Sheet			Income Statement		
Assets	= Liabilities	+ Owners' Equity <--	Net income	= Revenues	– Expenses
	Payroll Taxes Payable + 4,800				Payroll Tax Expense - 4,800

b. Failure to make the accrual resulted in an understatement of expense and an overstatement of net income. On the 3/31/96 balance sheet, current liabilities are understated and retained earnings is overstated.

7-3. c.

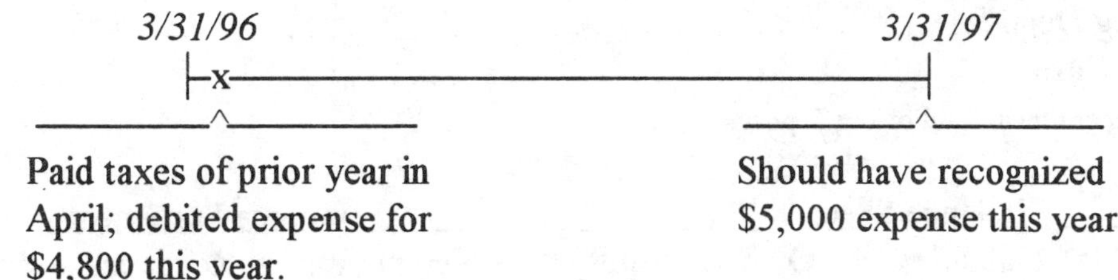

Effect on net income for year ended 3/31/97:
Expense is too high by amount applicable to prior year: $4,800
Expense is too low by accrual *not* made this year: $5,000
Net effect is that expense this year is $200 too low, and profits this year are $200 too high.

Effect on the 3/31/97 balance sheet:
Current liabilities are $5,000 understated, and retained earnings is $5,000 overstated.

7-5. *December 31:*

	Dr.	Cr.
Dr. Advertising Expense ($2,700,000 * 60% * 5%)	$81,000	
Cr. Estimated Liability for Advertising Allowance		$81,000

To accrue the estimated liability for advertising allowances offered.

Balance Sheet					Income Statement			
Assets	=	Liabilities	+	Owners' Equity <--	Net income	=	Revenues	- Expenses
		Estimated Liability for Advertising Allowance + 81,000						Advertising Expense - 81,000

7-7. a. Warranty Expense = ($3,600,000 sales * 0.4% estimated warranty expense) = $14,400

b.

Estimated Warranty Liability, 1/1/96 balance	$35,200
Less: Actual warranty costs during 1996	(15,600)
Add: Warranty Expense accrued during 1996	14,400
Estimated Warranty Liability, 12/31/96 balance	$34,000

7-9. a. Keg deposits are a current liability on the balance sheet because they are amounts that are likely to be paid within a year.

7-9. b. Dr. Keg Deposits $15
Cr. Cash $15
To record the refund of keg deposits.

Balance Sheet					Income Statement			
Assets	=	Liabilities	+	Owners' Equity <--	Net income =	Revenues	–	Expenses
Cash – 15		Keg Deposits – 15						

c. The Keg Deposits liability for the 200 kegs (200 * $15 = $3,000) should be eliminated with a debit; an income statement account (such as Keg Deposits Revenue) should be credited.

Dr. Keg Deposits $3,000
Cr. Keg Deposits Revenue $3,000
To eliminate the liability for unreturned kegs.

Balance Sheet					Income Statement			
Assets	=	Liabilities	+	Owners' Equity <--	Net income =	Revenues	–	Expenses
		Keg Deposits – 3,000				Keg Deposits Revenue + 3,000		

d. The cost of kegs purchased would be capitalized in a long-lived asset account, and then be depreciated over the kegs' estimated useful life. The net book value of kegs removed from service, or lost (as in part *c*) would be removed from the asset and recorded as an expense (or a loss).

Dr. Keg Expense (or Loss on Unreturned Kegs) . . . . $ xxx
Dr. Accumulated Depreciation xxx
Cr. Kegs (or other appropriate asset account) . . . . $ xxx
To record a loss for the net book value of unreturned kegs.

Balance Sheet					Income Statement			
Assets	=	Liabilities	+	Owners' Equity <--	Net income =	Revenues	–	Expenses
– Kegs + Accumulated Depreciation								– Keg Expense *(or Loss on Unreturned Kegs)*

7-11. a. *September 1, 1996*

Dr. Cash	$4,200	
Cr. Unearned Rent Revenue		$4,200

To record the receipt a six-month advance rent payment.

Each month-end:

Dr. Unearned Rent Revenue	$700	
Cr. Rent Revenue		$700

To record a reduction in the liability account for rent earned each month.

Balance Sheet				Income Statement		
Assets =	Liabilities +	Owners' Equity	<--	Net income =	Revenues -	Expenses
Cash + 4,200	Unearned Rent Revenue + 4,200					
	Unearned Rent Revenue - 700				Rent Revenue + 700	

b. At December 31, 1996, 4 months of rent has been earned, and 2 months remains to be earned. So 2/6 of the original premium of $4,200, or $1,400 is unearned rent and will be shown on the December 31 balance sheet as a current liability.

c. At a rate of $700 per month, the receipt of an 18-month rent prepayment would have been for $12,600. The unearned amount at December 31, 1996, is $9,800 ($700 per month for the next 14 months). Only $8,400 ($700 * 12 months) of this amount is a current liability, because of the one-year time frame for current liabilities. Thus, $1,400 ($700 * 2 months) of the unearned amount is technically a noncurrent liability.

7-13. a. The market interest rate is higher than the stated interest rate, so the bonds will sell for less than their face amount. The higher the discount rate (i.e., market interest rate), the lower the *present value* of cash flows associated with the bond (for interest payments and principal) becomes.

b.

Dr. Cash	$1,080,000	
Cr. Bonds Payable		$1,000,000
Cr. Premium on Bonds Payable		80,000

To record the issuance of bonds payable at a premium.

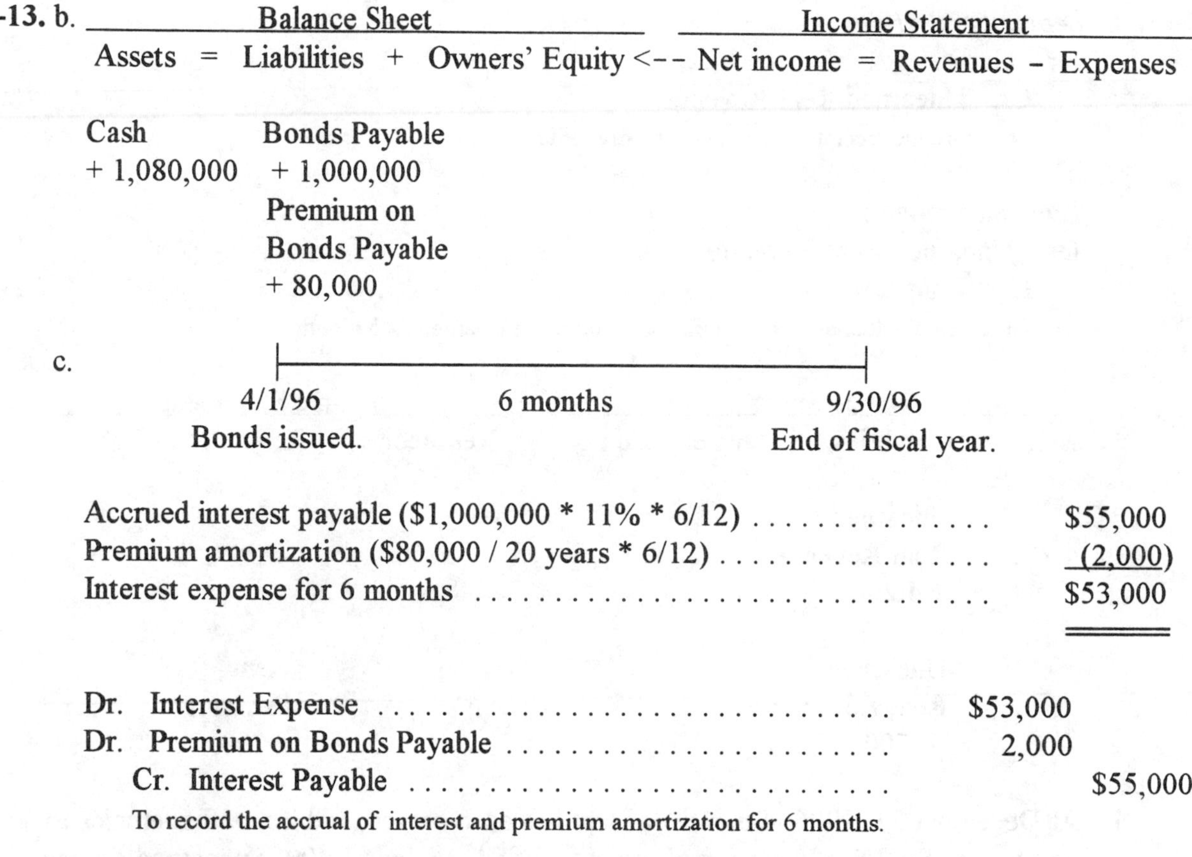

7-13. b.

Balance Sheet					Income Statement				
Assets	=	Liabilities	+	Owners' Equity	<-- Net income	=	Revenues	-	Expenses
Cash + 1,080,000		Bonds Payable + 1,000,000 Premium on Bonds Payable + 80,000							

c.

4/1/96 Bonds issued. — 6 months — 9/30/96 End of fiscal year.

Accrued interest payable ($1,000,000 * 11% * 6/12)	$55,000
Premium amortization ($80,000 / 20 years * 6/12)	(2,000)
Interest expense for 6 months	$53,000

Dr. Interest Expense	$53,000	
Dr. Premium on Bonds Payable	2,000	
Cr. Interest Payable		$55,000

To record the accrual of interest and premium amortization for 6 months.

7-15. The semiannual interest on the bonds = 10% stated rate * $5,000 face amount * 6/12 = **$250**
The remaining term of the bonds is 12 years, or **24 semiannual periods.**
The semiannual market interest rate is = 8% * 6/12 = **4%**

The present value of an interest annuity of $250 for 24 periods at 4% =
$250 * 15.2470 = **$3,811.75**
The present value of the maturity value of $5,000 in 24 periods at 4% =
$5,000 * 0.3901 = **$1,950.50**
The market value of the bonds = PV of interest + PV of maturity value =
$3,811.75 + $1,950.50 = **$5,762.25**

7-17. a. Because the exchange ratio is five shares of common stock to one bond, bondholders would be interested in converting the bonds to common stock if the market price per share of common stock was at least 20% (or more) of the market price per bond. For example, when the bonds were issued on January 1, 1980 at their $1,000 face amount, the market rate of interest and the stated rate were both 12%, and the market price per bond was $1,000. At that time, bondholders would not have been willing to convert their bonds unless the common stock was trading at price of $200 per share or more.

7-17. b. ***Solution approach:*** Upon exercise of the conversion feature, the bonds have been retired and thus the Bonds Payable account must be reduced by the carrying value of $1,000 per bond retired (there was no discount or premium). Common stock has been issued for $215 per share and should be recorded in the usual way. The difference is a loss on the early retirement of bonds of $75 per bond retired (or $15 per share of common stock issued) because the company gave more in exchange for the bonds ($215 per share * 5 shares equals $1,075) than the carrying value of the bonds ($1,000 per bond).

Dr. Bonds Payable (400 bonds * $1,000 per bond)	$400,000	
Dr. Loss on Early Retirement of Bonds #	30,000	
Cr. Common Stock (400 bonds * 5 shares * $10 par) . . .		$ 20,000
Cr. Additional Paid-In Capital (400 * 5 * $205 per share)		410,000

To record the conversion of bonds to common stock at a loss.

For financial reporting purposes, gains and losses on the early retirement of debt are reported as "extraordinary items" on the income statement, and are shown *net* of their tax effects. The accounting for extraordinary items is discussed in Chapter 9.

Balance Sheet				Income Statement		
Assets	= Liabilities	+ Owners' Equity	<-- Net income	= Revenues	- Expenses	
	Bonds Payable - 400,000	Common Stock + 20,000 Additional Paid-In Capital + 410,000				Loss on Early Retirement of Bonds - 30,000

7-19. a. Annual interest payment = $40 million * 11% = **$4,400,000**

b. The bonds were issued at a discount because market interest rates were more than the stated rate when the bonds were issued. The higher the discount rate (i.e., the market interest rate), the lower the *present value* of cash flows for interest payments and principal (i.e., the lower the bond's selling price).

c. Interest expense will be more than the interest paid because the amortization of bond discount will increase interest expense.

7-21. a. The semiannual interest payments on the bonds =
14% stated rate * $3,000,000 face amount * 6/12 = **$210,000**

The term of the bonds is 10 years, or **20 semiannual periods.**

The semiannual market interest rate is = 12% * 6/12 = **6%**

7-21. a. ***(Continued)***

The present value of an annuity of $210,000 for 20 periods at 6% =
$210,000 * 11.4699 = **$2,408,679**

The present value of the maturity value of $3,000,000 in 20 periods at 6% =
$3,000,000 * 0.3118 = **$935,400**

The proceeds (issue price) of the bonds = PV of interest + PV of maturity value =
$2,408,679 + $935,400 = **$3,344,079**

b. The semiannual discount amortization, straight-line basis = $50,000 / 20 periods = **$2,500**

	Dr.	Cr.
Dr. Interest Expense	$212,500	
Cr. Cash		$210,000
Cr. Discount on Bonds Payable		2,500

To record the semiannual cash payment and amortization of discount.

Balance Sheet				Income Statement		
Assets	= Liabilities	+ Owners' Equity	<-- Net income	= Revenues	-	Expenses
Cash - 210,000	Discount on Bonds Payable + 2,500					Interest Expense - 212,500

c. Discount on bonds payable is amortized with a credit, and thus increases interest expense. Under the straight-line basis, the amount of discount amortization is the same each period. Under the compound (or *effective*) interest method, the amount of discount amortization increases each period. Thus, interest expense under the compound method will be lower in the early years of the bond's life, and higher in the later years, as compared to interest expense under the straight-line method of amortization.

Rationale of compound interest method: Interest expense under the compound interest method is calculated by multiplying the carrying value of the bond (face amount minus the unamortized discount) by the market rate of interest. This amount is then compared to the *cash payment* required (the face amount multiplied by the stated rate). Any difference between interest expense and the required cash payment represents the amortization of discount for the period. Because the carrying value of the bond *increases* over the life of the bond as discount is amortized, the *amount* of discount amortization also increases each period, causing interest expense to be higher each period. Thus, as compared to the straight-line basis, interest expense under the compound method will be lower in the first year.

7-23. The principal risk associated with financial leverage is that a decrease in the entity's operating income could result in a decrease in cash flows and an inability to make interest and required principal payments on the debt. A second risk is that as the amount of debt increases, lenders require a higher interest rate to compensate for the additional risk they are taking.

7-25. The amount of deferred income taxes has risen steadily because the excess of accelerated tax depreciation over straight-line book depreciation on recent asset additions exceeds the excess of book depreciation over tax depreciation for older asset additions. This occurs because as the company grows over time, asset additions increase in amount, and over time the cost of replacement assets rises because of inflation.

7-27.

Transaction/ Adjustment	*Current Assets*	*Current Liabilities*	*Long-Term Debt*	*Net Income*
a.		+ 867		- 867
b.		+ 170		- 170
c.		+ 1,700		- 1,700
d.			+ 615	- 615
e.	- 1,240	- 1,240		
f.		+ 1,500		- 1,500

a. Dr. Wages Expense	$867	
Cr. Wages Payable		$867
b. Dr. Interest Expense	$170	
Cr. Interest Payable		$170
c. Dr. Interest Expense ($240,000 * 8.5% * 1/12)	$1,700	
Cr. Interest Payable		$1,700
d. Dr. Interest Expense	$615	
Cr. Discount on Bonds Payable		$615
e. Dr. Estimated Warranty Liability	$1,240	
Cr. Cash		$410
Cr. Parts Inventory		830
f. Dr. Sales	$1,500	
Cr. Unearned Revenues		$1,500

7-29.

Transaction/ Adjustment	*Current Assets*	*Noncurrent Assets*	*Current Liabilities*	*Noncurrent Liabilities*	*Owners' Equity*	*Net Income*
a.			Income Taxes Payable + 500	Deferred Income Taxes + 200		Income Tax Expense – 700
b.	Cash + 4,950			Bonds Payable + 5,000 Discount on Bonds Payable – 50		
c.	Cash – 3,000	Land + 3,000				
d.	Inventory – 64		Estimated Warranty Liability – 64			
e.	Cash + 19,400		Notes Payable + 20,000 Discount on Notes Payable – 600			
f.			Current Maturities of Long-Term Debt + 35,000	Serial Bonds Payable – 35,000		

		Dr.	Cr.
a.	Dr. Income Tax Expense	$700	
	Cr. Income Taxes Payable		$500
	Cr. Deferred Income Taxes		200
b.	Dr. Cash	$4,950	
	Dr. Discount on Bonds Payable	50	
	Cr. Bonds Payable		$5,000
c.	Dr. Land	$3,000	
	Cr. Cash		$3,000
d.	Dr. Estimated Warranty Liability	$64	
	Cr. Inventory		$64

7-29. e. Dr. Cash ($20,000 – ($20,000 * 12% * 3/12)) $19,400
Dr. Discount on Notes Payable ($20,000 * 12% * 3/12) 600
Cr. Notes Payable $20,000

f. Dr. Serial Bonds Payable $35,000
Cr. Current Maturities of Long-Term Debt $35,000

Chapter 8. Accounting for and Presentation of Owners' Equity

8-1.

	A	=	L	+	PIC (OE)	+	RE (OE)	
Beginning	$ (4)		$ (3)		(1)		(2)	$520,000 OE
Changes	+260,000		+21,000		+40,000		+ (7)	Net income
							–55,000	Dividends
Ending	(5)	=	$234,000	+	$175,000	+	(6)	

Steps:
1. $175,000 – $40,000 = $135,000
2. $520,000 – $135,000 = $385,000
3. $234,000 – $21,000 = $213,000
4. $213,000 + $520,000 = $733,000
5. $733,000 + $260,000 = $993,000
6. $993,000 – $234,000 – $175,000 = $584,000
7. $385,000 + Net income – $55,000 = $584,000
   Net income = **$254,000**

Short-cut approach:
$260,000 = + $21,000 + $40,000
+ Net income – $55,000

Net income = **$254,000**

8-3. Prepare the retained earnings portion of a statement of changes in owners' equity for the year ended December 31, 1996:

Retained earnings, December 31, 1995	$346,400
Add: Net income for the year	56,900
Less: Dividends for the year	(32,500)
Retained earnings, December 31, 1996	**$370,800**

8-5. a. Balance sheet amount equals number of shares issued * par value.
1,400,000 shares * $5 = **$7,000,000**

b. Cash dividends are paid on shares outstanding.
1,250,000 shares * $0.15 = **$187,500**

c. Treasury stock accounts for the difference between shares issued and shares outstanding.

8-7. a.

Number of shares issued	161,522
Less: Number of shares in treasury	(43,373)
Number of shares outstanding	118,149
Dividend requirement per share	* $3.75
Total annual dividends required to be paid	**$443,058.75**

b.

Dividend per share (6% * $40 par value)	$2.40
Number of shares outstanding	73,621
Total annual dividends required to be paid	**$176,690.40**

c.

Dividend per share (11.4% * $100 stated value)	$11.40
Number of shares outstanding	37,600
Total annual dividends required to be paid	**$428,640**

8-9. Preferred dividends for 1994, 1995, and 1996 would have to be paid before a dividend on the common stock could be paid. Annual dividend = $6.50 * 22,000 shares = $143,000
Dividends for 3 years = 3 * $143,000 = **$429,000**

8-11. a. *January 1, 1996:*

Dr. Cash ((150,000 @ $19) + (60,000 @ $122))	$10,170,000	
Cr. Common Stock (150,000 shares @ $19 per share)		$2,850,000
Cr. Preferred Stock (60,000 shares @ $100 per share)		6,000,000
Cr. Additional Paid-In Capital—Preferred (60,000 @ $22)		1,320,000

To record stock issuances.

December 28, 1997:

Dr. Retained Earnings	$1,800,000	
Cr. Dividends Payable		$1,800,000

To record the declaration of dividends.

February 12, 1998:

Dr. Dividends Payable	$1,800,000	
Cr. Cash		$1,800,000

To record the payment of dividends.

8-11. a. ***(Continued)***

Balance Sheet			Income Statement
Assets =	Liabilities +	Owners' Equity <--	Net income = Revenues - Expenses

To record stock issuances:

Assets	Liabilities	Owners' Equity
Cash + 10,170,000		Common Stock + 2,850,000 Preferred Stock + 6,000,000 Additional Paid-In Capital + 1,320,000

To record the declaration of dividends:

Assets	Liabilities	Owners' Equity
	Dividends Payable + 1,800,000	Retained Earnings - 1,800,000

To record the payment of dividends:

Assets	Liabilities	Owners' Equity
Cash - 1,800,000	Dividends Payable - 1,800,000	

b. Preferred shareholders are entitled to one year of dividends in arrears (for 1996), as well as their current year preference (for 1997). 60,000 shares * $100 par per share * 9.5% = $570,000 per year * 2 years = **$1,140,000**

8-13. a. February 21 is the declaration date. Because this is a regular dividend of the same amount as prior dividends, the stock price would not be significantly affected.

b. March 12 is the ex-dividend date. On this date the market price of the stock is likely to fall by the amount of the dividend because purchasers will not receive the dividend.

c. March 15 is the record date. The market price of the stock should not be affected because for a publicly traded stock it is the ex-dividend date that affects who receives the dividend.

d. March 30 is the payment date. The market price of the stock should not be affected because the corporation is merely paying a liability (dividends payable).

8-15. To declare a dividend, the firm must have retained earnings and enough cash to pay the dividend. Of course the board of directors must approve a dividend.

8-17. If the company can reinvest its retained earnings at a higher ROI than I could earn on the money paid to me in dividends, I would prefer that the company *not* pay a cash dividend. If I needed current income from my investment, I would want cash dividends. *(Note: Refer to the ROI and ROE calculations for Microsoft Corporation in Problem 3-12 for an example of a company that does not, and should not, declare cash dividends.)* As a common stock investor, I don't really care whether or not the company issues a stock dividend, because a stock dividend doesn't change my equity in the company, or the total market value of my investment, or the company's ability to earn a return on my investment.

8-19. a. A 2-for-1 split means that for every share now owned, the stockholder will own 2 shares. Thus, I will own 200 shares.

b. Because there are now twice as many shares of stock outstanding, and the financial condition of the company hasn't changed, the market price per share will be half of what it was. The total market value of my investment will not have changed.

8-21. a. *May 4, 1996*

Dr. Treasury Stock	$14,600	
Cr. Cash		$14,600

To record the purchase of 800 shares of treasury stock @ $18.25 per share.

b. *June 15, 1996*

Dr. Retained Earnings (36,200 – 800 = 35,400 shares * $0.35)	$12,390	
Cr. Cash		$12,390

To record the declaration and payment of a cash dividend.

c. *September 11, 1996*

Dr. Cash (600 shares @ $19.50)	$11,700	
Cr. Treasury Stock (600 shares @ $18.25)		$10,950
Cr. Additional Paid-In Capital (600 shares @ $1.25)		750

To record the sale of 600 shares of treasury stock @ $19.50 per share.

Balance Sheet			Income Statement	
Assets =	Liabilities +	Owners' Equity <--	Net income =	Revenues – Expenses

To record the purchase of 800 shares of treasury stock @ $18.25 per share:

Assets	Liabilities	Owners' Equity
Cash		Treasury Stock
– 14,600		– 14,600

To record the declaration and payment of a cash dividend:

Assets	Liabilities	Owners' Equity
Cash		Retained Earnings
– 12,390		– 12,390

8-21.

Balance Sheet			Income Statement
Assets = Liabilities +	Owners' Equity <--		Net income = Revenues − Expenses

To record the sale of 600 shares of treasury stock @ $19.50 per share.

Cash	Treasury Stock
+ 11,700	+ 10,950
	Additional Paid-in Capital
	+ 750

8-23.

Transaction	*Cash*	*Other Assets*	*Liabilities*	*Paid-in Capital*	*Retained Earnings*	*Treasury Stock **	*Net Income*
a.	+			+			
b.			+		−		
c.	−					+	
d.				+	−		
e.		+		+			
f.	+			+		−	

g. No entry is required for a stock split.

* Note that an increase in treasury stock (for a purchase transaction such as item *c*) *decreases total owners' equity*, and a decrease in treasury stock (for a sale transaction such as item *f*) *increases total owners' equity*. The effects shown are with respect to the Treasury Stock account, which is a contra owners' equity account.

a. Dr. Cash	$xxx	
Cr. Preferred Stock		$xxx
b. Dr. Retained Earnings	$xxx	
Cr. Dividends Payable		$xxx
c. Dr. Treasury Stock	$xxx	
Cr. Cash		$xxx
d. Dr. Retained Earnings	$xxx	
Cr. Common Stock		$xxx
Cr. Additional Paid-In Capital		???
e. Dr. Land	$xxx	
Cr. Common Stock		$xxx
Cr. Additional Paid-In Capital		???
f. Dr. Cash	$xxx	
Cr. Treasury Stock		$xxx
Cr. Additional Paid-In Capital		xxx

8-25.

Transaction	*Cash*	*Other Assets*	*Liabilities*	*Paid-in Capital*	*Retained Earnings*	*Treasury Stock **	*Net Income*
a.	+ 90,000			+ 90,000			
b.		+ 40,000		+ 40,000			
c.	- 3,200				- 3,200		
d.	- 4,750					+ 4,750	
e.			+ 6,713		- 6,713		
f.	+ 2,600			+ 130		- 2,470	
g.				+ 28,350	- 28,350		

h. No entry is required for a stock split.

* Note that an increase in treasury stock (for a purchase transaction such as item *d*) *decreases total owners' equity*, and a decrease in treasury stock (for a sale transaction such as item *f*) *increases total owners' equity.* The effects shown are with respect to the Treasury Stock account, which is a contra owners' equity account.

a. Dr. Cash	$90,000	
Cr. Common Stock (5,000 shares @ $1 per share)		$ 5,000
Cr. Additional Paid-In Capital (5,000 shares @ $17 per share)		85,000
b. Dr. Land and Building	$40,000	
Cr. Preferred Stock (1,000 shares @ $40 per share)		$40,000
c. Dr. Retained Earnings (1,000 shares * $40 per share * 8%)	$3,200	
Cr. Cash		$3,200
d. Dr. Treasury Stock ($4,750 / 250 shares = $19 per share)	$4,750	
Cr. Cash		$4,750
e. Dr. Retained Earnings (40,000 + 5,000 – 250 = 44,750 shares)	$6,713	
Cr. Dividends Payable (44,750 shares outstanding * $0.15 per share)		$6,713
f. Dr. Cash (130 shares @ $20 per share)	$2,600	
Cr. Treasury Stock (130 shares @ $19 per share)		$2,470
Cr. Additional Paid-In Capital (130 shares @ $1 per share)		130
g. Dr. Retained Earnings (45,000 shares *issued* * 3% = 1,350)	$28,350	
Cr. Common Stock (1,350 dividend shares @ $1 per share)		$ 1,350
Cr. Additional Paid-In Capital (1,350 shares @ $20 per share)		27,000

8-27. a. Annual dividend per share (12% * $60) .... $ 7.20
Number of shares outstanding 1,500
Annual dividend requirement **$10,800**

8-27. b. Balance sheet amount = ($60 par value * 1,500 shares issued) = **$90,000**

c. Number of shares issued = ($240,000 balance sheet amount / $8 par value) = **30,000**
Number of shares outstanding = (30,000 shares issued – 2,000 treasury shares) = **28,000**

d.

	Common Stock	Additional Paid-in Capital
November 30, 1996	$240,000	$540,000
January 1, 1996	(210,000)	(468,750)
Increase	$ 30,000	$ 71,250

Number of shares sold = ($30,000 increase in common stock / $8 par value) = **3,750**
Selling price per share = (($30,000 increase in common stock + $71,250 increase in additional paid-in capital) / 3,750 shares sold) = **$27 per share.**

e. Treasury stock was resold at a price greater than its cost.

f.

Retained earnings, January 1, 1996	$90,300
Add: Net income	24,000
Less: Preferred stock dividends *(see answer to part a)*	(10,800)
Less: Common stock dividends	?
Retained earnings, December 31, 1996	$97,000

Solving for the unknown amount, common stock dividends = **$6,500**

8-29. a. Par value per share of preferred stock = ($1,440,000 balance sheet amount / 24,000 shares issued) = **$60 par value per share.**
Preferred stock dividend percentage = ($4.50 dividend per share / $60 par value per share) = **7.5 %**

b. Balance sheet amount for common stock = (820,000 shares issued * $5 par value per share) = **$4,100,000** (shown as $4,100).

c. Average issue price of common stock = (($4,100,000 common stock + $5,740,000 additional paid-in capital) / 820,000 shares issued) = **$12 per share issued.**

d. Treasury shares = (820,000 issued shares – 750,000 outstanding shares) = **70,000**

e. Balance sheet amount for treasury shares = (70,000 shares * $18 per share) = **$1,260,000** (shown as $1,260).

8-29. f.

Preferred stock	$ 1,440,000
Common stock	4,100,000
Additional paid-in capital	5,740,000
Retained earnings	?
Treasury stock	(1,260,000)
Total stockholders' equity	$15,000,000

Solving for the unknown amount, retained earnings = **$4,980,000** (shown as $4,980).

g.

Retained earnings, July 1, 1994	$4,800,000
Add: Net income	288,000
Less: Preferred stock dividends (24,000 shares outstanding * $4.50 per share)	(108,000)
Retained earnings, June 30, 1995	**$4,980,000**

Chapter 9. The Income Statement and the Statement of Cash Flows

9-1.

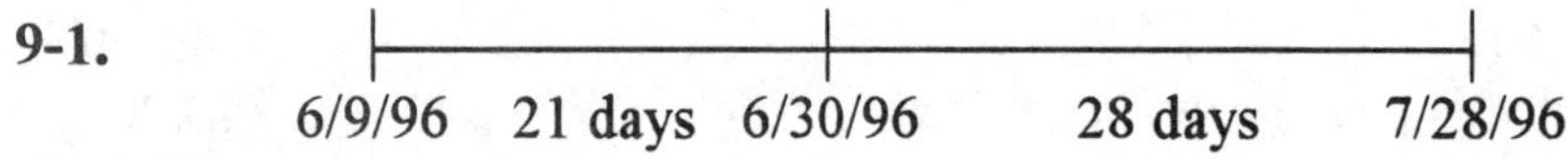

a. For the year end June 30, 1996, recognize 21/49 of summer school tuition, because that proportion of the summer session occurs within the first fiscal year. Summer session expenses will be accrued or deferred (i.e., recognized as incurred), so an appropriate matching of revenue and expense will occur in each fiscal year.

Amount of revenue for the year ended June 30, 1996 = (21/49 * $112,000) = **$48,000**

b. No. Revenues and expenses would still be allocated to each fiscal year to achieve the most appropriate matching (based on when revenues are *earned* and when expenses are *incurred*). Since revenues are earned as services are provided, the critical event is the offering of classes rather than the university's tuition refund policy. Thus, the amounts calculated in part *a* would still result in the most meaningful financial statements for each fiscal year.

9-3. A sale could be billed before the product is shipped. Internal controls would involve a policy of not billing until after shipment, and procedures that required a copy of the shipping record to be received in the billing department before the sales invoice could be mailed to the customer.

9-5. ***Solution approach:*** Use the cost of goods sold model with hypothetical data that are the same except for the item in error:

	"Error"	*"Correct"*
Beginning inventory	$100,000	$100,000
Add: Purchases	300,000	300,000
Goods available for sale	$400,000	$400,000
Less: Ending inventory	(125,000)	(75,000)
Cost of goods sold	$275,000	$325,000

The overstatement of ending inventory causes cost of good sold to be too low, so gross profit and operating income are too high, or overstated, by $50,000.

9-7. a.

	1994	*1993*	*1992*
Net sales *($ millions)*	$2,752.7	$2,525.4	$2,549.8
Cost of good sold *($ millions)*	(1,904.7)	(1,819.2)	(1,903.8)
Gross profit *($ millions)*	$ 848.0	$ 706.2	$ 646.0
Gross profit ratio	30.8%	28.0%	25.3%

b. Use the estimated gross profit ratio for 1993 of 28.0%, because it approximates the three-year average:

Net sales *($ millions)*	$845.0
Cost of goods sold (72%)	(608.4)
Gross profit (28%)	$236.6

9-9. I would prefer to have operating income data, because this describes how well management has done operating the business. Net income is important, but includes non-operating items such as discontinued operations, other income and expense, and extraordinary items. Thus, trends in operating income data are more likely to reflect the firm's ability to generate future earnings than are trends in net income data.

9-11. a.

Net sales	$644,000
Cost of goods sold	(368,000)
Gross profit	$276,000
General and administrative expenses	(143,000)
Advertising expense	(45,000)
Other selling expenses	(13,000)
Operating income	$ 75,000

9-11. b. *Note:* Since Manahan Co. did not report any interest expense, or other income or expense, the operating income amount calculated in part *a* also represents the firm's "Income before taxes."

Income before taxes (operating income)	$ 75,000
Income tax expense	(26,000)
Earnings before extraordinary item	$ 49,000
Extraordinary loss from flood, net of taxes of $35,000	(105,000)
Net loss	**$ (56,000)**

9-13. ***Solution approach:*** Calculate ending inventory in the cost of goods sold model for the high (33%) and low (30%) gross profit ratios, and select the ratio that gives the highest ending inventory.

	Gross Profit Ratio				*Calculation*
	33%		*30%*		*Sequence*
Sales		$142,680		$142,680	Given
Cost of goods sold:					
Beginning inventory	$ 63,590		$ 63,590		Given
Add: Purchases	118,652		118,652		Given
Goods available for sale	$182,242		$182,242		
Less: Ending inventory	(86,646)		(82,366)		3rd
Cost of goods sold		$(95,596)		$(99,876)	2nd
Gross profit		$ 47,084		$ 42,804	1st *

* Gross profit percentage multiplied by sales.

Franklin Co.'s management would argue for using a 33% gross profit ratio for 1996 to the date of the tornado, because the higher the gross profit ratio, the higher the estimated ending inventory lost in the storm, and the greater the insurance claim.

9-15.

	Net income	$473,700
	Less: Dividends required on preferred stock (38,000 shares * $4.50 per share)	(171,000)
	Net income available for common stockholders	$302,700
/	Number of common share outstanding	105,200
=	Earnings per share	**$2.88**

9-17. Armstrong uses the multiple-step format. The multiple-step format seems easier to read and interpret, because of the intermediate captions and subtotals.

9-19. a. ($760,000 sales on account + $24,000 decrease in accounts receivable) = **$784,000** source of cash. Since accounts receivable decreased during the year, more accounts were collected in cash than were created by credit sales.

Accounts Receivable

Beginning balance	$???	Cash collections	
Sales on account	$760,000	from customers	**$784,000**
Ending balance	$??? – $24,000		

b. ($148,000 income tax expense + $34,000 decrease in income taxes payable) = **$182,000** use of cash. Tax payments exceeded the current year's income tax expense because the payable account decreased.

Income Taxes Payable

		Beginning balance	$???
Cash payments for taxes	**$182,000**	Income tax expense	$148,000
		Ending balance	$??? – $34,000

c. ($408,000 cost of goods sold + $14,000 increase in inventory – $19,000 increase in accounts payable) = **$403,000** use of cash. Cost of goods sold reflects inventory uses. Inventory purchases were greater than inventory uses because inventory increased during the year, but part of the inventory purchases were not paid for in cash because accounts payable also increased during the year.

Inventory

Beginning balance	$???		
Inventory purchases	$422,000	Cost of goods sold	$408,000
Ending balance	$??? + $14,000		

Accounts Payable

		Beginning balance	$???
Cash payments for purchases (to suppliers)	**$403,000**	Inventory purchases	$422,000
		Ending balance	$??? + $19,000

d. ($240,000 increase in net book value + $190,000 depreciation expense) = **$430,000** use of cash. Since depreciation is an expense that does not affect cash, the amount of cash paid to purchase new buildings exceeded the increase in net book value. *(Note: In some years, a firm may spend an enormous amount of cash to acquire new buildings and equipment, yet still report a decrease in net book value.)*

9-19. d. ***(Continued)***

Buildings, net of Accumulated Depreciation			
Beginning balance	$???		
Purchase of buildings	**$430,000**	Depreciation expense	$190,000
Ending balance	$??? + $240,000		

9-21. a. ***Cash flows from operating activities:***

Net income	$420,000
Add (deduct) items not affecting cash:	
Depreciation and amortization expense	320,000
Accounts receivable decrease	45,000
Inventory increase	(20,000)
Accounts payable decrease	(10,000)
Income tax payable increase	35,000
Net cash provided by operating activities	**$790,000**

b. Net income is based on accrual accounting, and revenues may be *earned* before or after cash is received. Likewise, expenses may be *incurred* before or after cash payments are made. Thus, net income and cash flows provided by operations may differ because of the *timing* of cash receipts and payments. In addition the timing issue, other adjustments to net income may be necessary to add back non-cash expenses (such as depreciation and amortization), or to remove the effects of non-operating transactions (such as the gains and losses from the sale of long-term assets). To adjust net income for timing differences, changes during the year in non-cash working capital items (i.e., current assets other than cash, and current liabilities) must be considered. If a current asset account increases or if a current liability account decreases during the year, the cash account balance is assumed to have decreased. If a current asset account decreases or if a current liability account increases, the cash account balance is assumed to have increased. *(Note: Review Business Procedure Capsule 20 on pages 347-348 in the text if you are having difficulty understanding these adjustments.)*

9-23. ***Solution approach:*** Prepare a statement of cash flows—direct method *(see Exhibit 9-8)*.

a. **Cash flows from operating activities:**	***(in millions)***
Cash collected from customers	$1,350
Interest and taxes paid	(90)
Cash paid to suppliers and employees	(810)
Net cash provided by operating activities	$ 450

9-23. b. **Cash flows from investing activities:**

Purchase of land and buildings	$(170)
Proceeds from the sale of equipment	40
Net cash used for investing activities	**$(130)**

c. **Cash flows from financing activities:**

Payment of long-term debt	$ (220)
Issuance of preferred stock	300
Cash dividends declared and paid	(340)
Net cash used for financing activities	**$(260)**
d. Net increase in cash for the year	**$ 60**

9-25. a.

Net earnings	$ 63.5 million
Depreciation and amortization	130.0 million
Loss from restructuring activities	89.9 million
Cash provided by the three most significant operating sources	**$ 283.4** million

b.

Purchases of property, plant and equipment	$(117.6) million
Proceeds from sale of land and facilities	10.3 million
Net cash used for investing activities	**$(107.3)** million

c.

Decrease in short-term debt	$ (114.9) million
Reduction of long-term debt	(9.2) million
Cash used to reduce debt	**$(124.1)** million

d. Dividends totaled $63.8 million.

e.

ARMSTRONG WORLD INDUSTRIES, INC.
Condensed Statement of Cash Flows
For the Year Ended December 31, 1993

	(in millions)
Cash flows from operating activities:	
Net earnings	$ 63.5
Depreciation and amortization	130.0
Loss from restructuring activities	89.9
All other operating activities (net)	7.8
Net cash provided by operating activities	**$ 291.2**
Cash flows from investing activities:	
Purchases of property, plant and equipment	$ (117.6)
Proceeds from sale of land and facilities	10.3
Net cash used for investing activities	**$(107.3)**

9-25. e. ***(Continued)***

Cash flows from financing activities:

Decrease in short-term debt	$ (114.9)
Reduction of long-term debt	(9.2)
Cash dividends paid	(63.8)
All other financing activities (including exchange rate effect—net)	(2.1)
Net cash used for financing activities	$(190.0)
Net cash decrease for the year	$ (6.1)

9-29. a.

HOEMAN, INC.
Balance Sheets
December 31, 1996, and 1995

Assets

	1996	*1995*
Current assets:		
Cash	$ 52,000	$ 46,000
Accounts receivable	(1)	134,000
Inventory	156,000	176,000
Total current assets	$ (2)	$ 356,000
Land	(3)	140,000
Buildings	(4)	290,000
Less: Accumulated depreciation	(120,000)	(105,000)
Total land & buildings	$ (5)	$ 325,000
Total assets	$ (6)	$ 681,000

Liabilities

Current liabilities:		
Note payable	$ 155,000	$ 124,000
Accounts payable	(7)	197,000
Total current liabilities	$ 322,000	$ 321,000
Long-term debt	$ (11)	$ 139,000

Owners' Equity

Common stock	$ 50,000	$ 45,000
Retained earnings	(9)	176,000
Total owners' equity	$ (10)	$ 221,000
Total liabilities and owners' equity	$ (8)	$ 681,000

9-29. a. ***(Continued)***

Calculations:

1. \$134,000 – \$10,000 = \$124,000
2. \$52,000 + \$124,000 + \$156,000 = \$332,000
3. Land is carried at historical cost = \$140,000
4. \$290,000 + \$125,000 = \$415,000
5. \$140,000 + \$415,000 – \$120,000 = \$435,000
6. \$332,000 + \$435,000 = \$767,000
7. \$322,000 – \$155,000 = \$167,000
8. Same as total assets = \$767,000
9. \$176,000 + \$94,000 – \$67,000 = \$203,000
10. \$50,000 + \$203,000 = \$253,000
11. \$767,000 – \$253,000 – \$322,000 = \$192,000

b.

HOEMAN, INC.
Statement of Cash Flows
For the Year Ended December 31, 1996

Cash flows from operating activities:	
Net income	\$ 94,000
Add (deduct) items not affecting cash:	
Depreciation expense	15,000
Decrease in accounts receivable	10,000
Decrease in inventory	20,000
Increase in notes payable	31,000
Decrease in accounts payable	(30,000)
Net cash provided by operating activities	**\$ 140,000**
Cash flows from investing activities:	
Cash paid to acquire new buildings	**\$(125,000)**
Cash flows from financing activities:	
Cash received from issuance of long-term debt	\$ 53,000
Cash received from issuance of common stock	5,000
Payment of cash dividends on common stock	(67,000)
Net cash used for financing activities	**(9,000)**
Net increase in cash for the year	**\$ 6,000**

Chapter 10. Explanatory Notes and Other Financial Information

10-1. Class discussion can focus on the importance of these items to a reader's full understanding of the company's financial statements (financial position, results of operations, and cash flows).

10-3.

ROI	=	MARGIN	x	TURNOVER
OPERATING PROFIT / AVERAGE IDENTIFIABLE ASSETS	=	OPERATING PROFIT / NET TRADE SALES	x	NET TRADE SALES / AVERAGE IDENTIFIABLE ASSETS

(Note: Average identifiable assets cannot be determined for 1992 because 1991 data are not reported. Thus, the ROI and turnover calculations shown below in the 1992 column are based on year-end assets, and the results shown in the 1993 and 1994 columns are based on average assets. To increase the accuracy of the trend comparison, Armstrong's 1993 annual report could be referred to for the 1991 data.)

ARMSTRONG WORLD INDUSTRIES, INC.
Trend of ROI by Industry Segments

Industry Products:	***1994***	***1993***	***1992***
Net trade sales	$312.2	$297.7	$319.8
Operating profit	41.2	27.2	29.7
Identifiable assets	234.8	207.9	197.0
Margin	13.2%	9.1%	9.3%
Turnover	1.41	1.47	1.62
ROI	18.6%	13.4%	15.1%

Building Products:	***1994***	***1993***	***1992***
Net trade sales	$630.0	$586.7	$656.7
Operating profit	86.8	18.8	(19.3)
Identifiable assets	478.1	483.0	500.3
Margin	13.8%	3.2%	(2.9)%
Turnover	1.31	1.19	1.31
ROI	18.1%	3.8%	(3.9)%

Furniture:			
Net trade sales	$526.8	$449.7	$438.4
Operating profit	38.6	24.1	5.8
Identifiable assets	245.2	234.6	238.7

10-3. ***(Continued)***

	1994	*1993*	*1992*
Margin	7.3%	5.4%	1.3%
Turnover	2.20	1.90	1.84
ROI	16.1%	10.2%	2.4%

10-5. a. Original earnings per share is $3.12. To reflect a 3 for 1 stock split, divide by 3.
Adjusted EPS = **$1.04**

b. For 1997, 1995 earnings per share as adjusted in 1996 will have to be adjusted again by dividing by 2. Adjusted EPS for 1995, to be reported in 1997 = $1.04 / 2 = **$0.52**

c. To reflect a 10% stock dividend, divide unadjusted earnings per share by 1.10.
Adjusted EPS = $3.12 / 1.10 = **$2.84**

10-7.

Earnings per share, as restated	$0.60
Multiply by 2 to reflect 2 for 1 stock split	$1.20
Multiply by 1.05 to reflect 5% stock dividend	**$1.26**
Proof: Original earnings per share	$1.26
Adjust for stock split (divide by 2)	$0.63
Adjust for 5% stock dividend (divide by 1.05)	$0.60

10-9. The auditors' opinion is that the identified financial statements *present fairly, in all material respects* (emphasis added), the financial position, results of operations, and cash flows in conformity with generally accepted accounting principles. Thus, the auditor does guarantee that the statements are free from *immaterial* errors or that they present *perfectly.*

10-11. a. 1. Net sales = **$2,752.7 million**
2. Income for operations = **$333.2 million**
3. Net earnings per share of common stock—primary =**$5.22**
4. Purchases of property, plant and equipment = **$148.3 million**
5. Number of shareholders (at year-end) = **7,473**

b. 1. Research and development costs = **$57.4 million** *(page 28)*
2. Interest and dividends income = **$3.7 million** *(page 28)*
3. Total pension cost = **$(10.2) million** *(page 29 in the first table shown—the negative amount at the bottom of the table represents the total pension credit, rather than cost)*
4. Machinery and equipment = **$1,523.8 million** *(page 32)*
5. Goodwill = **$67.4 million** *(page 33)*
6. Raw materials and supplies = **$78.9 million** *(page 32)*
7. Total taxes for the year = **$180.9 million** *(page 31)*
8. Cash dividends paid to preferred stockholders = **$19.0 million** *(page 38)*
9. Net sales during the second quarter of 1994 = **$689.3 million** *(page 44)*
10. Net trade sales in Europe for the year = **$483.4 million** *(page 36)*

Chapter 11. Financial Statement Analysis

11-1. a. 1. Income statement (or statement of operations).
2. Net income (or net earnings).
3. Earnings per share of common stock.
4. Statement of changes in owners' (or stockholders') equity.
5. Retained earnings.
6. Owners' (or stockholders') equity.
7. Working capital.
8. Owners' (or stockholders') equity.

b. 1. **ROI** = **MARGIN** x **TURNOVER**

$$\frac{\textbf{OPERATING INCOME}}{\textbf{AVERAGE TOTAL ASSETS}} = \frac{\textbf{OPERATING INCOME}}{\textbf{SALES}} \times \frac{\textbf{SALES}}{\textbf{AVERAGE TOTAL ASSETS}}$$

Margin = ($498 operating profit / $8,251 sales) = **6.0%**
Turnover = Sales / ((Total assets less current liabilities + Current liabilities) / 2)
= $8,521 / [(($4,873 + $2,758) + ($4,289 + $2,472)) / 2] = **1.15**
ROI = (6.0% Margin * 1.15 Turnover) = **6.9%**

2. ROE = (Net income / Average owners' equity) = (Profit / Average ownership)
= $350 / (($3,565 + $3,149) / 2) = **10.4%**

c. 1. Average day's sales = ($8,251 annual sales / 365 days) = $22.6 million
Number of days' sales in accounts receivable = ($2,174 accounts receivable / $22.6 average day's sales) = **96.2 days**
2. Inventory turnover = Cost of goods sold / Average inventory
= $6,253 / (($1,323 + $1,211) / 2) = **4.9 times**
3. Plant and equipment turnover = Sales / Average plant and equipment
= Sales / ((Buildings, machinery, and equipment + Land) / 2)
= $8,251 / [(($2,467 + $96) + ($2,431 + $97)) / 2] = **3.2 times**

d. 1. Debt/equity ratio= ($1,287 long-term debt / $3,565 ownership) = **36.1%**
2. Debt ratio = ($1,287 long-term debt / ($1,287 long-term debt + $3,565 ownership)) = **26.5%**
3. Times interest earned = (Earnings before interest and taxes / Interest expense)
= ($498 operating profit / $209) = **2.4 times**

e. 1. Price/earning ratio = (Market price per share / Earning per share)
= ($42.00 / $3.51 profit per share of common stock after extraordinary tax benefit) = **12.0**

11-1. e. 2. Dividend payout ratio = (Dividends per share / Earning per share)
= ($0.50 dividends paid per share of common stock / $3.51 profit per share of common stock after extraordinary tax benefit) = **14.2%**

3. Dividend yield = (Dividends per share / Market price per share)
= ($0.50 dividends paid per share of common stock / $42.00) = **1.2%**

11-3. Key data would be the recent (3-5 year) trend in earnings per share, cash dividends per share, market price, and P/E ratio. These data would be in tabular and graphic format. Market price would be noted weekly. Quarterly and annual data to note are earnings and dividend trends. The sell/hold/buy decision is based on stock price performance relative to the price objective established from analysis of the above data.

11-5.

ARMSTRONG WORLD INDUSTRIES, INC., AND SUBSIDIARIES
Common Size Balance Sheet
December 31, 1993

Total current assets	33.2%
Property, plant and equipment, (net)	53.9
Other noncurrent assets	12.9
Total assets	100.0%
Total current liabilities	22.6%
Total noncurrent liabilities	47.9
Total shareholders' equity	29.5
Total liabilities and shareholders' equity	100.0%

11-9. ***Note to the Student:*** *This problem is based on Armstrong's 1993 data because most of these same ratios for 1994 are presented in the chapter (in exhibits and the related text discussion). This problem can be used as a review, or to help you understand how the numbers in the exhibits were calculated. (Some of these ratios are also reported in the nine-year summary on page 52.)*

a. 1. Margin = ($63.5 net earnings / $2,525.4 net sales) = **2.5%**
Turnover = Sales / Average total assets = $2,525.4 / (($2,009.8 + $1,929.3) / 2) = **1.28**
ROI = (2.5% margin * 1.28 turnover) = **3.2%**

2. ROE = Net earnings / Average owners' equity
= $63.5 / (($569.2 + $569.5) / 2) = **11.2%**

3. Price/earnings ratio = ($53¼ market value per common share / $1.32 primary earnings per share) = **40.3**

11-9. a. 4. Dividend yield = ($1.20 dividends per common share / $53¼ market value per common share) = **2.3%**

5. Dividend payout ratio = ($1.20 dividends per common share / $1.32 primary earnings per share) = **90.9%**

b. 1. Working capital = ($640.4 current assets – $436.3 current liabilities) = **$204.1 million**

2. Current ratio = ($640.4 current assets / $436.3 current liabilities) = **1.47**

3. Acid-test ratio = (($9.1 cash and cash equivalent + $283.5 accounts and notes receivable) / $436.3 current liabilities) = **0.67**

c. 1. Average day's sales = ($2,525.4 annual net sales / 365 days) = $6.919 million

Number of days' sales in accounts receivable = ($283.5 accounts receivable / $6.919 average day's sales) = **41.0 days**

2. Average day's cost of goods sold = ($1,819.2 annual cost of goods sold / 365 days) = $4.984 million

Number of days' sales in inventory = ($286.2 inventory / $4.984 average day's cost of goods sold) = **57.4 days**

(Note: For the turnover calculations shown in parts c.3. and c.4. below, year-end balances are used for accounts and notes receivable, and for inventory, instead of average balances because the 1992 balance sheet data is not reported in the 1994 annual report. For part c.5., the 1992 balance is reported in the nine-year summary.)

3. Accounts and notes receivable turnover = Sales / Average accounts and notes receivable = ($2,525.4 / $283.5 year-end balance) = **8.9 times**

4. Inventory turnover = Cost of goods sold / Average inventory = ($1,819.2 / $286.2 year-end balance) = **6.4 times**

5. Net property, plant and equipment turnover = Sales / Average property, plant and equipment = $2,525.4 / (($1,039.1 + $1,072.0) / 2) = **2.4 times**

d. 1. Debt ratio = (Total liabilities / Total liabilities and shareholders' equity) = (($436.3 total current liabilities + $923.5 total noncurrent liabilities) / $1,929.3 total liabilities and shareholders' equity) = **70.5%**

2. Debt/equity ratio= (Total liabilities / Total shareholders' equity) = (($436.3 total current liabilities + $923.5 total noncurrent liabilities) / $569.5 total shareholders' equity) = **239%**

3. Times interest earned = (Earnings before interest and taxes / Interest expense) = ($122.7 operating income / $38.0) = **3.3 times**

11-9. e. 1. Net sales per employee = ($2,525,400,000 net sales / 21,682 average number of employees—continuing businesses) = **$116,474**

2. Operating income per employee = ($122,700,000 operating income / 21,682 average number of employees—continuing businesses) = **$5,659**

11-11. a. ***Campbell's Soup:*** Accounts receivable turnover = Sales / Average accounts receivable = $6,586 / (($557 + $646) / 2) = **10.9 times**

General Mills: Accounts receivable turnover = Sales / Average accounts receivable = $8,135 / (($292 + $287) / 2) = **28.1 times**

b. ***Campbell's Soup:*** Average day's sales = ($6,586 sales / 365 days) = $18.044 million

Number of days' sales in accounts receivable = ($646 accounts receivable / $18.044 average days' sales) = **35.8 days**

General Mills: Average day's sales = ($8,135 sales / 365 days) = $22.288 million

Number of days' sales in accounts receivable = ($287 accounts receivable / $22.288 average days' sales) = **12.9 days**

c. General Mills has an unusually fast collection cycle for its accounts receivables, which could be caused by a number of factors. First, it is possible that a substantial amount of the firm's reported sales were made on a *cash basis* (the footnote disclosures in the annual report may provide this information). If this were the case, then the accounts receivable turnover of 28.1 would be overstated, and the firm's collection cycle would be much longer than 12.9 days. General Mills probably makes most of its credit sales on a wholesale basis, and it possible that the firm offers a cash discount that is so high that its customers (buying in large volume) simply cannot refuse. The results for Campbell's Soup are certainly within the ordinary range of expectation, although they may seem poor by comparison.

11-13. a.

	RJR Nabisco	***Sara Lee Corporation***
Working Capital:		
Current assets	$ 4,349	$ 4,469
- Current liabilities	(5,550)	(4,919)
= Working capital	**$(1,201)**	**$ (450)**
Current Ratio:		
Current assets	$4,349	$4,469
/ Current liabilities	5,550	4,919
= Current ratio	**0.78**	**0.91**

11-13. a. ***(Continued)***

Acid-Test Ratio:

Cash and equivalents	$ 409	$ 189
+ Accounts and notes receivable	934	1,472
= Total (quick assets)	$1,343	$1,661
/ Current liabilities	5,550	4,919
= Acid-test ratio	**0.24**	**0.34**

b. Sara Lee may sell a greater proportion of goods *on account* than does RJR Nabisco. The credit terms (i.e., cash discounts) offered by Sara Lee may not be as favorable as those offered by Nabisco, so customers would not be as likely to make prompt payments. Sara Lee may allow customers a greater period of time to make payments (perhaps 60 days instead of 30 days), and Sara Lee may have a more liberal credit approval policy than does Nabisco.

c. Sara Lee's current maturities of long-term debt is extremely low relative to the amount shown for Nabisco. This suggests that Sara Lee does not have as much long-term debt as does Nabisco, and would need to finance its long-term asset growth with relatively more short-term debt (principally notes payable). *(Note: Sara Lee reported $1,496 million of long-term debt on July 2, 1994, and RJR Nabisco reported $8,883 million of long-term debt on its December 31, 1994 balance sheet.)*

d. Both firms report negative working capital and have extremely low acid-test ratios because inventories account for more than half of their current assets. Thus, neither firm is in a strong liquidity position. Based on the ratio results, Sara Lee appears to be in a better position. However, Sara Lee has very little cash relative to Nabisco, and it carries considerably more accounts and notes receivable—so it has a greater concern with collectibility than does Nabisco. Although Nabisco has more cash and fewer accounts and notes payable, it also has an obligation to pay $1.97 billion within the next year to reduce its long-term debt. Thus, Nabisco may need to borrow additional funds on a long-term basis to meet this current obligation.

Chapter 12. Managerial/Cost Accounting and Cost Classifications

12-1.

	Product				
	Direct	*Indirect*	*Period*	*Variable*	*Fixed*
Wages of assembly-line workers	x			x	
Depreciation—plant equipment		x			x
Glue and thread		x		x	
Shipping costs			x	x	
Raw materials handling costs		x		x	
Salary of public relations manager			x		x
Production run setup costs		x		x	
Plant utilities		x		x	x
Electricity cost of retail stores			x	x	x
Research and development expenses			x	x	x

Note: The last three items are each likely to have a mixed cost behavior pattern.

12-3. a. *Raw material:* cotton/ wool/ rayon used for jersey, or material used for team emblems.
b. *Direct labor:* wages of production-line machine operator.
c. *Variable manufacturing overhead:* plant utilities costs, or indirect materials (i.e., thread).
d. *Fixed manufacturing overhead:* depreciation of machinery, or property taxes on plant.
e. *Fixed administrative expense:* salaries of administrative officers.
f. *Indirect selling expense:* advertising costs.
g. *Variable, direct selling expense:* shipping costs.

12-5. a. *Differential cost:* What costs will differ if a friend comes along?
b. *Allocated cost:* How to allocate? Based on number of people, weight, number of suitcases, or what?
c. *Sunk cost:* What costs have already been incurred and cannot be recovered, even if you don't make the trip?
d. *Opportunity cost:* What are other opportunities for you to earn revenue? What is the cost of alternative travel for your classmate?

12-7. a. Predetermined overhead application rate = ($784,000 estimated total overhead cost / 140,000 estimated direct labor hours) = **$5.60 per direct labor hour.**

b. ***Total cost for 450 pairs of shoes produced:***

Raw materials	$ 8,190
Direct labor (270 direct labor hours * $9.60 per hour)	2,592
Overhead (270 direct labor hours * $5.60 predetermined rate)	1,512
Total manufacturing cost	$12,294

12-7. b. ***(Continued)***
Cost per pair of shoes produced = ($12,294 total cost / 450 pairs) = **$27.32 per pair.**
c. Cost of shoes sold = (370 pairs * $27.32 per pair) = **$10,108.40**
Cost of shoes in inventory = (80 pairs * $27.32 per pair) = **$2,185.60**

12-9. a. Predetermined overhead application rate $9.70 per machine hour
= (Estimated overhead costs / estimated activity of 8,400 machine hours)
= ? / 8,400 machine hours = **$81,480 estimated overhead.**

b.

Actual overhead incurred	$ 81,480
Overhead applied (8,200 machine hours @ $9.70 per hour)	(79,540)
Overhead was **underapplied** by	**$ 1,940**

c. Most of the products made during the year are sold during the same year. Thus, the overapplied or underapplied overhead for the year will be transferred to cost of goods sold in the income statement because most of it would have ended up there anyway if the "correct" overhead application rate had been used.

12-11. ***Total cost for 250 ties produced:***

Raw materials	$ 820.00
Direct labor (32 direct labor hours)	208.00
Overhead applied based on raw materials ($820 * 215%)	1,763.00
Overhead applied based on direct labor hours (32 hours * $3.10)	99.20
Total manufacturing cost	$ 2,890.20

Cost per tie produced = $2,890.20 / 250 ties = **$11.5608 per unit**

12-13. a. Total manufacturing cost = (Direct materials + Direct labor + Manufacturing overhead)

Direct materials		$3,500,000
Direct labor (160,000 hours * $20 per hour)		3,200,000
Manufacturing overhead:		
Materials handling ($1.50 per part * 275,000 parts used)	$ 412,500	
Milling and grinding ($11.00 per machine hour * 95,000 hours)	1,045,000	
Assembly and inspection ($5.00 per labor hour * 160,000 hours)	800,000	
Testing ($3.00 per unit * 50,000 units tested)	150,000	2,407,500
Total manufacturing cost		**$9,107,500**

Cost per unit produced = $9,107,500 / 50,000 units = **$182.15 per unit**

12-13. b. The activity based costing approach is likely to provide better information for manufacturing managers because overhead costs are applied based on the activities that *cause* the incurrance of cost (i.e., cost drivers). Thus, management attention will be directed to the critical activities that can be controlled to improve the firm's operating performance. ABC systems also produce more accurate product costing information, which can lead to better decision making.

12-15. a. Total cost = ($240 fixed cost + ($0.06 variable cost per mile * 1,146 miles)) = **$308.76**

b. No, it would not be meaningful to calculate an average cost per mile, because that would involve unitizing the fixed expenses, and they do not behave on a per mile basis. Whatever average cost per mile were calculated would be valid only for the number of miles used in the calculation. An average cost for any other number of miles driven would be different, because the fixed expenses per mile would decrease for each additional mile driven.

12-17. a.

Raw materials	$25,720
Direct labor	18,930
Variable manufacturing overhead	14,570
Total variable costs	$59,220
Fixed manufacturing overhead	10,320
Total manufacturing cost	$69,540

Direct (or variable cost) per spatula = $59,220 / 20,000 = **$2.961 per unit**
Absorption cost per spatula = $69,540 / 20,000 = **$3.477 per unit**

b. The fixed cost per spatula = ($3.477 – $2.961) = $0.516 per unit. (This can also be calculated as: $10,320 / 20,000 units = $0.516). Thus, the total fixed cost associated with 3,800 spatulas in inventory = (3,800 * $0.516) = **$1,960.80**

Under absorption costing an additional $1,960.80 would be in inventory. Under direct (or variable) costing, this amount would be in cost of goods sold. Thus, under direct (or variable) costing, gross profit would be $1,960.80 *less* than under absorption costing.

c. Total cost = $10,320 fixed cost + $2.961 variable cost per spatula produced.
The cost of making an additional 100 spatulas = (100 * $2.961) = **$296.10**

12-19. a.

Absorption cost per calculator	$ 9.65
Less: Fixed manufacturing overhead per calculator ($32,400 / 7,200)	(4.50)
Direct (or variable) cost per calculator	$ 5.15

12-19. b. Change in inventory = (900 calculators * $4.50 per unit) = **$4,050** *more* cost of goods sold released to the income statement this month under direct (or variable) costing than under absorption costing. Thus, net income under direct (or variable) costing will be $4,050 *lower* than under absorption.

c. Total cost = $32,400 fixed cost + $5.15 variable cost per calculator produced.

12-21. a.

Raw materials	$ 36,800
Direct labor	79,300
Manufacturing overhead	47,200
Total manufacturing cost #	$163,300

Since there was no information about the Work in Process Inventory account, it can be assumed that there was no change in the balance of this account. Thus, the cost of goods manufactured is equal to the total manufacturing cost incurred during March.

Cost per unit produced = $163,300 / 3,800 units = **$42.9737 per unit**

b. Cost of goods sold = (3,500 units @ $42.9737) = **$150,408**

c. The difference between the cost of goods manufactured and cost of goods sold is in the Finished Goods Inventory account on the balance sheet. Finished Goods Inventory value = (300 units @ $42.9737) = **$12,892**

12-23. a.

Raw materials	$25,300
Direct labor	20,800
Manufacturing overhead (1,600 hours * $ 22 per direct labor hour)	35,200
Total manufacturing cost #	$81,300

Since there was no information about the Work in Process Inventory account, it can be assumed that there was no change in the balance of this account. Thus, the cost of goods manufactured is equal to the total manufacturing cost incurred during January.

Cost per unit produced = $81,300 / 2,100 units = **$38.714 per unit**

b. Finished goods inventory = (200 units @ $38.714) = **$7,742.86**

c. This cost information is not very useful for planning and control purposes because it includes unitized fixed manufacturing overhead.

12-25. ***Solution approach:*** Using T-accounts, enter the beginning and ending balance amounts, and the debits which are given, then solve for the credits: raw materials used, cost of goods manufactured, and cost of goods sold.

Raw Materials

Debit		Credit	
Beg. Bal.	$ 45,790	Used	$209,940
Purchases	217,580		
End. Bal.	$53,430		

Work in Process

Debit		Credit
Beg. Bal.	$ 18,930	**Cost of Goods Manufactured $774,930**
Raw Mat.	209,940	
Dir. Labor	392,100	
Mfg. Ovrhd.	169,300	
End. Bal.	$ 15,340	

Finished Goods

Debit		Credit
Beg. Bal.	$ 63,650	**Cost of Goods Sold $770,300**
Cost of Goods Manufactured	774,930	
End. Bal.	$ 68,280	

Chapter 13. Cost–Volume–Profit Analysis

13-1. a. ***Solution approach:*** First, calculate variable cost per unit in February and use the same per unit cost for April. Second, fixed cost will be the same for each month. Third, with knowledge of total costs for April, and variable and fixed costs for April, solve for mixed costs for April.

	February	***April***
Activity	5,000 units	7,000 units
Costs:		
Variable ($10,000 / 5,000 units = $2 per unit)	$10,000	$14,000
Fixed (same total amount each month)	30,000	30,000
Mixed (Total costs – (Variable + Fixed))	20,000	**24,000**
Total	$60,000	$68,000

b. Variable rate = (High $ – Low $) / (High units – Low units)
= ($24,000 – $20,000) / (7,000 – 5,000) = **$2.00 per unit**

Total mixed cost = Fixed cost + Variable cost
$24,000 = ? + ($2.00 * 7,000 units)
? = $10,000

Cost formula = (Fixed cost + Variable rate) = **($10,000 + $2.00 per unit)**

Proof at 5,000 units: Mixed cost = $10,000 + ($2.00 * 5,000 units) = $20,000

13-3. a.

Revenues (8,000 units * $4 per unit)		$32,000
Variable expenses:		
Cost of goods sold (8,000 units * $ 2.10 per unit)	$16,800	
Selling expenses (8,000 unit * $0.10 per unit)	800	
Administrative expenses (8,000 units * $0.20 per unit) . . .	1,600	
Total variable expenses		19,200
Contribution margin		$12,800
Fixed expenses:		
Cost of goods sold	$6,000	
Selling expenses	1,200	
Administrative expenses	4,000	
Total fixed expenses		11,200
Operating income		$ 1,600

b. Contribution margin per unit = Total CM / Volume = $12,800 / 8,000 units = **$1.60**

Alternative approach: CM per unit = Selling price per unit – Variable expense per unit
= $4.00 – $2.40 = **$1.60 per unit**

Contribution margin ratio = CM / Revenues
= $12,800 / $32,000 = **40%**

Alternative approach: CM ratio = CM per unit / Selling price per unit
= $1.60 / $4.00 = **40%**

c. 1. ***Volume of 12,000 units:***

	Per Unit	*	*Volume*	=	*Total*	*%*
Revenue	$ 4.00					100%
Variable Expense	2.40					60
Contribution Margin	$ 1.60	*	12,000	=	$ 19,200	40%
Fixed Expense					(11,200)	
Operating Income					**$ 8,000**	

Alternative approach: 4,000 more units sold @ $1.60 CM per unit = $6,400 increase in contribution margin and operating income. Present operating income is $1,600, so new operating income will be $8,000.

13-3. c. 2. ***Volume of 4,000 units:***

	Per Unit	*	*Volume*	=	*Total*	%
Revenue	$ 4.00					100%
Variable Expense	2.40					60
Contribution Margin	$ 1.60	*	4,000	=	$ 6,400	40%
Fixed Expense (no change)					(11,200)	
Operating Loss					**$ (4,800)**	

Alternative approach: Operating income decreases by $6,400 (4,000 units * $1.60 per unit) from present operating income of $1,600, causing an operating loss of $4,800.

d. 1. Use the contribution margin ratio of 40%. Revenue increase of $12,000 causes a $4,800 increase (40% * $12,000) in contribution margin and operating income. Operating income = $1,600 + $4,800 = **$6,400**

2. Revenue decrease of $7,000 causes a $2,800 decrease (40% * $7,000) in contribution margin and operating income. Operating income changes to a loss = $1,600 – $2,800 = **$(1,200)**

13-5. a.

Sales	$65,000
Variable expenses (80% * $65,000)	(52,000)
Contribution margin (20% $65,000)	$13,000
Fixed expenses	(18,000)
Operating loss	$(5,000)

Note: Operating loss remains the same, so Fixed expenses = ($13,000 Contribution margin + $5,000 Operating loss).

b.

Increase in sales (30% * $65,000)	$19,500
Contribution margin ratio	20%
Increase in contribution margin	$ 3,900
Previous operating loss	(5,000)
Adjusted operating loss	$(1,100)

Operating loss = $(5,000) + $3,900 = **$(1,100).** The increase in contribution margin is also a decrease in the operating loss, because fixed expenses do not change.

13-5. c. At break-even, contribution margin = fixed expenses = $18,000
Contribution margin = (20% contribution margin ratio * ??? sales) = $18,000
Sales = ($18,000 fixed expenses / 20% CM ratio) = $90,000 at break-even.

13-7. a.

	Per Unit	*	*Volume*	=	*Total*
Revenue	$ 15				
Variable Expense	9				
Contribution Margin	$ 6	*	5,400	=	$ 32,400
Fixed Expense					(27,000)
Operating Income					**$ 5,400**

b.

	Per Unit	*	*Volume*	=	*Total*
Revenue	$ 13				
Variable Expense	9				
Contribution Margin	$ 4	*	8,400	=	$ 33,600
Fixed Expense					(27,000)
Operating Income					**$ 6,600**

c. Does the increase in volume move fixed expenses into a new relevant range? Are variable expenses really linear?

d.

	Per Unit	*	*Volume*	=	*Total*
Revenue	$ 16				
Variable Expense	9				
Contribution Margin	$ 7	*	5,400	=	$ 37,800
Fixed Expense					(33,000)
Operating Income					**$ 4,800**

13-7. e. 1. ***Volume of 5,400 units per month:***

	Per Unit	*	Volume	=	Total
Revenue	$ 15.00				
Variable Expense	9.80				
Contribution Margin	$ 5.20	*	5,400	=	$ 28,080
Fixed Expense #					(22,800)
Operating Income					**$ 5,280**

# Current fixed expenses	$27,000
Decrease in fixed expenses (2 salespersons @ $2,500)	(5,000)
Increase in fixed expenses (2 salespersons @ $400)	800
Adjusted fixed expenses	$22,800

2. ***Volume of 6,000 units per month:***

	Per Unit	*	Volume	=	Total
Revenue	$ 15.00				
Variable Expense	9.80				
Contribution Margin	$ 5.20	*	6,000	=	$ 31,200
Fixed Expense					(22,800)
Operating Income					**$ 8,400**

f.

	Per Unit	*	Volume	=	Total
Revenue	$ 15				
Variable Expense	9				
Contribution Margin	$ 6	*	6,000	=	$ 36,000
Fixed Expense					(28,000)
Operating Income					**$ 8,000**

The sales force compensation plan change results in $400 more operating income than does the plan to increase advertising.

13-7. g.

	Per Unit	*	*Volume*	=	*Total*
Revenue	$ 15				
Variable Expense	9				
Contribution Margin	$ 6	*	?	=	$ 27,000
Fixed Expense					(27,000)
Operating Income					$ 0

At the break-even point, total contribution margin must equal total fixed expenses.
Break-even volume = ($6 contribution margin per unit * ??? volume) = $27,000

Thus, break-even volume = **4,500 units**

Total revenue = (4,500 units * $15 per unit) = **$67,500**

13-9. a. ***Current Operation:***

	Luxury	*Economy*	*Total*
Revenue	$20 * 10,000 = $200,000	$12 * 20,000 = $240,000	$440,000
Variable Expense	9	7	
Contribution Margin	$11 * 10,000 = $110,000	$ 5 * 20,000 = $100,000	$210,000
Fixed Expense			(70,000)
Operating Income			**$140,000**

Contribution margin ratio = $210,000 / $440,000 = **47.7%**

b. Break-even point revenues = Fixed expenses / Contribution margin ratio
= $70,000 / 47.7% = **$146,751**

c. Because sales mix might change. For example, if the company sold only the economy model, total contribution margin would equal the economy model contribution margin ratio ($5 / $12 = 41.7%) multiplied by the current break-even sales of $146,751, which equals $61,146. Note that this amount is less than the $70,000 of fixed expenses, so the firm would have to generate a higher sales volume to break even (because of the lower average contribution margin ratio).

13-9. d. ***Proposed Expansion:***

	Luxury	*Economy*	*Value*	*Total*
Rev.	$20 * 6,000 = $140,000	$12 * 17,000 = $204,000	$15 * 8,000 = $120,000	$464,000
V. E.	9	7	8	
C. M.	$11 * 6,000 = $ 66,000	$ 5 * 17,000 = $ 85,000	$ 7 * 8,000 = $ 56,000	$207,000
Fixed Expenses				(84,000)
Operating Income				**$123,000**

e. No. Based on this data analysis, adding the Value model would result in lower total operating income.

f. No. Although 2,000 more units of the Value model would increase total contribution margin and operating income by $14,000 (2,000 units @ $ 7 CM per unit), operating income would rise to $137,000, which is still less than under the current operation.

13-11. a. Use the model, enter the known data, and solve for the unknown.

	Per Unit	*	*Volume*	=	*Total*	*%*
Revenue	$?					100%
Variable Expense	7.80					
Contribution Margin	$?	*		=	$	35%

Variable expenses = 65% of selling price. Selling price = $7.80 / 65% = **$12.00**

b.

	Per Unit	*	*Volume*	=	*Total*	*%*
Revenue	$ 12.00					100%
Variable Expense	7.80					
Contribution Margin	$ 4.20	*	?	=	$?	35%
Fixed Expense					(15,000)	
Operating Income					$ 6,000	

Total contribution margin must be $21,000, divided by the contribution margin per unit of $4.20 gives **5,000** units of the new product that must be sold.

13-13. a.

	Per Unit	*	Volume	=	Total	%
Revenue	$ 1.25					100%
Variable Expense	0.35					28
Contribution Margin	$ 0.90	*	400	=	$ 360	72%
Fixed Expense					(120)	
Operating income from increased volume					$ 240	
Variable expenses of 600 cones given away, @ $0.35					(210)	
Net increase in operating income					**$ 30**	

b. Yes. Not only does the promotion itself result in increased operating income, but it is also likely that customers will purchase some other products (e.g., food and/or beverages) on which additional contribution margin will be earned.

13-15. a.

	Per Unit	*	Volume	=	Total	%
Revenue	$ 32					100.0%
Variable Expense	20					62.5
Contribution Margin	$ 12	*	4,100	=	$ 49,200	37.5%
Fixed Expense					(43,200)	
Operating Income					**$ 6,000**	

b.

	Per Unit	*	Volume	=	Total	%
Revenue	$ 32					100.0%
Variable Expense	20					62.5
Contribution Margin	$ 12	*	?	=	$ 43,200	37.5%
Fixed Expense					(43,200)	
Operating Income					$ 0	

Break-even volume = $43,200 / $12 per unit = **3,600 units**

Break-even revenues = 3,600 units * $32 per unit = **$115,200**

13-15. c. 1.

	Per Unit	*	*Volume*	=	*Total*	*%*
Revenue	$ 32					100.00%
Variable Expense	14					43.75
Contribution Margin	$ 18	*	4,100	=	$ 73,800	56.25%
Fixed Expense					(67,800)	
Operating Income					**$ 6,000**	

2.

	Per Unit	*	*Volume*	=	*Total*	*%*
Revenue	$ 32					100.00%
Variable Expense	14					43.75
Contribution Margin	$ 18	*	?	=	$ 67,800	56.25%
Fixed Expense					(67,800)	
Operating Income					$ 0	

Break-even volume = $67,800 / $18 = **3,767 units** (rounded)

Break-even revenues = 3,767 units * $32 = **$120,533** (rounded)

3. As sales volume moves above the break-even point, contribution margin and operating income will increase by a greater amount per unit sold than under the old cost structure.

4. The new cost structure has much more risk, because if sales volume declines, the impact on contribution margin and operating income will be greater than under the old cost structure.

13-17. a.

Raw materials per unit	$1.50
Direct labor per unit	1.50
Variable overhead per unit	2.00
Fixed overhead per unit	2.00 #
Total cost per unit	$7.00

The fixed overhead per unit is based on the total fixed overhead for the year of $100,000 divided by the current output of 50,000 units per year.

13-17. b. The above calculation includes an inappropriate unitization of fixed expenses. Unless the additional production of 30,000 units results in a movement to a new relevant range, total fixed expenses will not change.

c. The offer should be accepted because it would generate a contribution margin of $1 per unit (revenue of $6 per unit less variable cost of $5 per unit).

13-19. ***Pros:***

1. The sale will still generate a positive contribution margin ratio of 5%.
2. Saturn Candy Company will achieve goodwill with these customer and others concerned with corporate "social responsibility" issues.
3. The candy given to the children will increase brand awareness and could lead to greater sales in the future.
4. The Substance Abuse Awareness Club is a positive moral force in the community.

Cons:

1. Saturn Candy Company incurs an opportunity cost equal to the lost contribution margin if the candy could have been sold at the regular price.
2. When other customers learn of the discounted sale, they may ask for the same special price for other "worthy causes." Unless Saturn Candy Company develops a policy with some limits for this sort of special pricing, the company could lose control of its production cost per unit.
3. Special pricing transactions that are not based on quantity discounts may be in violation of federal price discrimination laws. Legal counsel should be consulted before agreeing to the special price.

Recommendation: An appropriate corporate policy and other safeguards concerning special order pricing arrangements should be developed, and the candy should be sold at the special price.

Chapter 14. Budgeting and Performance Reporting

14-1.

	May	*June*	*July*	*August*
Sales forecast in units	30,000	40,000	60,000	50,000
Beginning inventory			12,000	
Production			???	
Goods available for sale			70,000	
a. Less: Ending inventory #	(8,000)	(12,000)	(10,000)	
Number of units sold			60,000	

20% of next month's unit sales.

14-1. b. ***July production:***

12,000 + ??? – 10,000 = 60,000
Production = 58,000 units

14-3. a. Use the cost of goods sold model, and work from the bottom up and the top down:

Beginning inventory	1,000 medallions
Production	???
Goods available for sale	???
Less: Ending inventory	(800)
Quantity sold	2,000

Goods available for sale = 2,000 + 800 = 2,800 medallions
Production = 2,800 – 1,000 = **1,800 medallions**

b. Use the same approach, but notice that quantity used is a function of quantity produced from the production budget. Each medallion requires 2/3 of a yard of ribbon.

Beginning inventory	50 yards
Purchases	???
Raw materials available for use	???
Less: Ending inventory	(20)
Raw materials used in production (2/3 * 1,800 medallions)	1,200

Raw materials available for use = 1,200 + 20 = 1,220 yards
Purchases = 1,220 – 50 = **1,170 yards**

14-5. a. Use the raw material inventory/usage model:

	Quarter I	*Quarter II*
Beginning inventory	5,000	9,000
Add: Purchases	???	???
Raw materials available for use	???	???
Less: Ending inventory (25% of next quarter's usage)	(9,000)	(5,500)
Usage (2 ounces * number of gallons of product to be produced)	20,000	36,000
Working backwards (up the model):		
Raw materials available for use	29,000	41,500
Purchases (subtract beginning inventory)	**24,000**	**32,500**

b. Inventory provides a "cushion" for delivery delays or production needs in excess of the production forecast.

14-7.

	July	*August*	*September*
Sales forecast	$192,000	$215,000	$230,000
Cost of sales @ 78%	149,760	167,700	179,400

Purchases budget:		
Beginning inventory	$235,000	$251,550
Purchases	???	???
Cost of merchandise available for sale	???	???
Less: Ending inventory (1.5 * next month's cost of goods sold)	(251,550)	(269,100)
Cost of goods sold	$ 149,760	$ 167,700
Cost of merchandise available for sale = (Cost of goods sold + Ending inventory)	$ 401,310	$ 436,800
Purchases = (Cost of merchandise available for sale – Beginning inventory)	**$ 166,310**	**$ 185,250**

14-9.

	May	*June*	*July*	*August*
Sales forecast	$200,000	$300,000	$350,000	$250,000
Cash collections:				
20% of current month's sales			$ 70,000	$ 50,000
70% of prior month's sales			210,000	245,000
9% of second prior month's sales			18,000	27,000
Total cash collections budget			**$298,000**	**$322,000**

14-11. a.

	September	*October*
Sales forecast	$42,000	$54,000
Purchases budget	37,800	44,000
Operating expense budget	10,500	12,800

Beginning cash	**$40,000**
Cash receipts:	
August 31 accounts receivable	20,000
September sales	0
Total cash receipts	**$20,000**

14-11. a. ***Cash disbursements:***

August 31 accounts payable and accrued expenses	$24,000
September purchases (75% * $37,800)	28,350
September operating expenses (75% * $10,500)	7,875
Total cash disbursements	$60,225
Ending cash	$ (225)

b. QB Sportswear's management should try to accelerate the collection of accounts receivable, slow down the payment of accounts payable and accrued expenses, and/or negotiate a bank loan. If sales growth continues at a very high rate, they probably will need to secure some permanent financing through sale of bonds or stock.

14-13. a. The president's remark ignores the misleading result of arbitrarily allocated fixed expenses.

b.

Current net income of company		$10,000
Less: Lost contribution margin of Division B		(10,000)
Add: Division B direct fixed expenses that would be eliminated:		
Total Division B fixed expenses per report	$11,000	
Less: Allocated corporate ($21,000 / 3 divisions)	(7,000)	4,000
Company net income without Division B		$ 4,000

c. Never arbitrarily allocate fixed expenses!

14-15.

Item	*Original Budget (10,000 units)*	*Flexed Budget (11,000 units)*	*Actual Cost*	*Variance*
Direct Materials	$ 30,000	$ 33,000	$ 32,000	$1,000 F
Direct Labor	42,000	46,200	47,000	800 U
Variable Overhead	18,000	19,800	20,000	200 U
Fixed Overhead	33,000	33,000	34,000	1,000 U
Total	$123,000	$132,000	$133,000	$1,000 U

Note: The flexed budget amounts for variable expenses are calculated by multiplying the original budget amounts by 1.10 (11,000 units / 10,000 units). An alternative approach would be to compute the variable costs per unit based on original budget amounts (i.e., DM = $3.00, DL = $4.20, and VOH = $1.80). Per unit costs are then applied to actual activity to determine flexible budget amounts. Fixed expenses do not change as activity changes, so the fixed overhead amount is not flexed.

14-17. a. Cost formula = $3,800 + $2.70 per machine hour
Budget = $3,800 + ($2.70 * 3,700 machine hours) = **$13,790**

b. Flexed budget = $3,800 + ($2.70 * 3,580 machine hours) = **$13,466**

Chapter 15. Standard Costs and Variance Analysis

15-1. a. Costs for a "batch" of 10 quarts:

Triphate solution (11 quarts @ $0.30 per quart)	$3.30
Sobase granules (4 pounds @ $0.74 per pound)	2.96
Methage (2 ounces @ $1.20 per ounce)	2.40
Bottles (10 @ $0.12 each)	1.20
Total cost for 10 quarts	$9.86
Cost per quart ($9.86 / 10 quarts)	**$0.986**

b. Other factors to be considered:
1. Possible cost increases during coming year.
2. Spillage / spoilage / waste in the manufacturing process.

c. Expected labor costs for the most likely (or economical) production quantity would be determined, and then expressed on a per unit basis.

15-3. a.

Raw material cost	$2.83 per bushel
Direct labor and variable overhead	0.42 per bushel
Fixed overhead	0.35 per bushel
Total absorption cost	**$3.60 per bushel**

Each bushel yields 15 pounds of product. Cost per pound = $3.60 / 15 = **$0.24 per pound.**

b. This cost per pound is not very useful for management planning and control because it includes unitized fixed expenses, which do not behave on a per unit basis.

15-5. a. *Raw material purchase price variance:*
(Standard price – Actual price) * Actual quantity purchased
($5.00 – $4.95) * 7,400 pounds = **$370 F**

b. *Raw material usage variance:*
(Standard usage – Actual usage) * Standard price
((2,000 cases * 4 pounds) – 8,300 pounds) * $5.00 per pound = **$1,500 U**

15-5. c. *Direct labor rate variance:*
(Standard rate – Actual rate) * Actual hours
($13.00 – $13.50 #) * 5,800 hours = **$2,900 U**
Actual rate: $78,300 / 5,800 hours = $13.50

d. *Direct labor efficiency variance:*
(Standard hours – Actual hours) * Standard rate
((2,000 cases * 3 hours) – 5,800) * $13.00 = **$2,600 F**

e. *Variable overhead spending variance:*
(Standard rate – Actual rate) * Actual hours
($6.00 – $6.15 #) * 5,800 hours = **$870 U**
Actual rate: $35,670 / 5,800 hours = $6.15

f. *Variable overhead efficiency variance:*
(Standard hours – Actual hours) * Standard rate
((2,000 cases * 3 hours) – 5,800) * $6.00 = **$1,200 F**

Explanation of results: In order to create a favorable purchase price variance, the purchasing manager may have purchased lower-than-standard *quality* raw material inputs. This may have caused an excess amount of waste and spoilage, resulting in an unfavorable raw materials usage variance that *by far* exceeded the cost savings of $0.05 per pound. The unfavorable labor rate variance of $0.50 per hour may have been caused by using a more skilled and/or experienced workforce than was anticipated. However, this cost was largely offset by increased labor efficiency (i.e., less down-time, re-work). The favorable labor efficiency variance caused a favorable variable overhead efficiency variance because variable overhead is applied on the basis of direct labor hours.

15-7. a. Standard hours allowed = 3.5 hours * 24 tune-ups = 84 hours
Efficiency variance was 6 hours unfavorable, therefore actual hours = 84 + 6 = **90 hours.**

Standard labor cost allowed for actual hours ($15 per hour * 90 hours)	$1,350
Less: Favorable labor rate variance	(81)
Actual total labor cost	**$1,269**

Actual labor rate per hour = $1,269 / 90 hours = **$14.10 per hour**

b. Direct labor efficiency variance:
(Standard hours – Actual hours) * Standard rate
(84 – 90) * $15 = **$90 U**

15-7. c. Less skilled, lower paid workers took longer than standard to get the work done. Net variance is $9 U ($90 U - $81 F). This was not a good trade-off based on the variance. From a qualitative viewpoint, less skilled workers may not do as good of a job.

15-9. a. Purchase price variance = (Standard price - Actual price) * Actual quantity purchased = ($8.00 per board foot - ??? actual price) * 19,000 board feet purchased = $2,850 U. Thus, the purchase price per board foot was $0.15 U ($2,850 U / 19,000), or **$8.15.**

b. 1,500 units produced * 12 board feet per unit = **18,000 standard board feet allowed.**

c. Direct material usage variance = (Standard usage - Actual usage) * Standard price = (18,000 board feet allowed - 17,200 issued into production) * $8.00 per board foot = **$6,400 F**

d. The purchasing manager may have purchased higher-than-standard *quality* raw material inputs. This may have allowed Dutko, Inc., to reduce waste and spoilage, resulting in a favorable raw materials usage variance that more than offset the $0.15 per board foot unfavorable price variance. Based on the variances during November, this is a good trade-off for the management of Dutko, Inc., to make.

15-11. a.

	Original Budget	***Flexed Budget***	***Actual***	***Variance***
Direct labor	$1,800	$1,716 #	$1,888	$172 U

2,860 books / 20 books per hour = 143 standard hours allowed * $ 12 per hour = $1,716 flexed budget.

b. Direct labor efficiency variance = (143 standard hours - 160 actual hours) = **17 hours U.**

c. Direct labor rate variance = (Standard rate - Actual rate) * Actual hours = ($12 - ($1,888 / 160 hours)) * 160 hours = ($12 - $11.80) * 160 = **$32 F**

15-13. No. For example, management might be able to control results better if the labor efficiency variance is reported daily, in hours. The labor rate variance might be reported only weekly or monthly because labor rates are likely to be governed by contractual provisions that are not subject to short-term control. The reason for calculating variances is to encourage action to eliminate unfavorable variances and to capture favorable variances—not simply to assess blame. Thus, performance reporting systems should be designed to provide the most timely information (i.e., hourly, daily, weekly, or monthly) in the most appropriate manner (i.e., dollar amounts, quantities used, or hours worked) to the individuals within the organization who are in the best position to achieve the organization's objectives.

15-15. a. Raw material usage, and direct labor and variable overhead efficiency variances are in the aggregate about 15% of the total standard cost of goods produced. This indicates that the standards are not a very effective tool for controlling raw material, direct labor, and variable overhead costs.

b. The variances were favorable, so the standards are higher than actual costs incurred. Therefore, ending inventory values at standard costs will be higher than actual cost.

c. Use the 15% difference between standard and actual. Ending inventory should be reduced to 85% of standard cost to adjust it to actual cost. 85% * $158,780 = $134,963. The adjustment would be a $23,817 (15% * $158,780) reduction in ending inventory.

15-17. a.

	Simple	***Complex***
Work hours per day	7.5	7.5
Divided by: Standard processing time per claim (in hours)	0.75	2.5
Standard number of claims processed (per day per worker)	10.0	3.0
Multiplied by: Number of days in the month	20.0	20.0
Standard claims processed (per month per worker)	200.0	60.0
Claims processed	3,000	600
Standard number of workers required for the month	**15**	**10**

Thus, a total of **25** workers should have been available to process the April claims.

b.

Actual number of workers	27
Standard number of workers required for the month	25
Efficiency variance, in number of workers	**2 U**
Efficiency variance, in dollars (2 workers * $ 90 per day * 20 days)	**$3,600 U**

15-19. a. Predetermined overhead application rate $= \dfrac{\text{Estimated overhead \$}}{\text{Estimated activity}} = \dfrac{\$36{,}000}{(40{,}000 \text{ units} * 0.5 \text{ hours})}$

= $1.80 per machine hour

b. 39,000 units produced * 0.5 machine hours per unit = **19,500 machine hours allowed.**

c. Applied overhead = $1.80 * 19,500 hours = **$35,100**

d. ($37,000 actual overhead incurred – $35,100 overhead applied) = **$1,900 underapplied.**

e. ($36,000 budgeted overhead – $37,000 actual overhead) = **$1,000 U budget variance.**

((20,000 budgeted hours – 19,500 standard hours allowed for units produced) * $1.80 predetermined overhead application rate) = **$900 U volume variance.**

Chapter 16. Capital Budgeting

16-1. a.

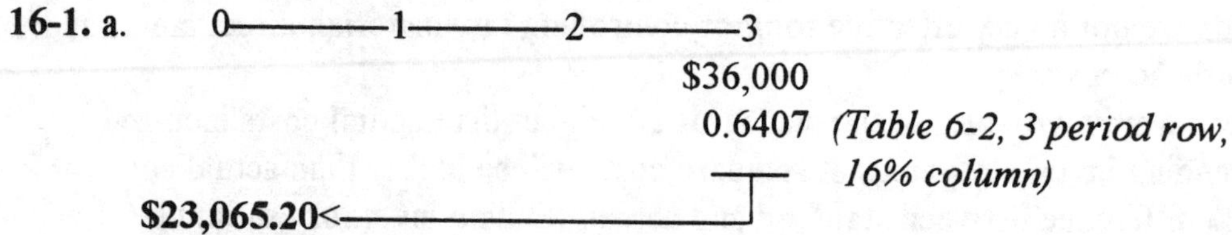

b. This is a future value problem, the opposite of present value. As shown in the diagram, $23,065.20 invested today at 16% interest compounded annually would grow to $36,000 in three years.

c. Less could be invested today because at a higher interest rate, more interest would be earned. This can be seen by calculating the present value of $36,000 in three years at an interest rate greater than 16%. As can be seen in Table 6-2, the present value factors are smaller as interest rates get higher.

16-3. a. If the investment is too high, the net present value will be too low.

b. If the cost of capital is too low, the net present value will be too high.

c. If the cash flows from the project are too high, the net present value will be too high.

d. If the number of years over which the project will generate cash flows is too low, the net present value will be too low.

16-5. a.

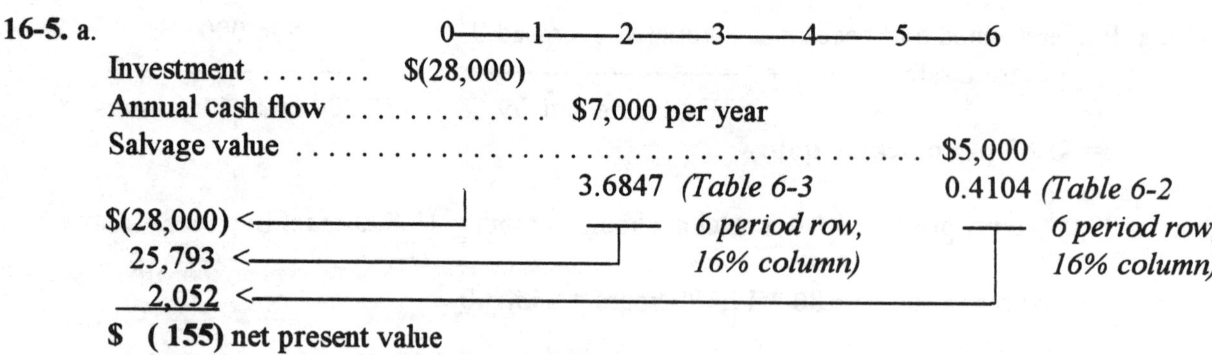

b. Because the net present value is negative, the internal rate of return on this project will be lower than the cost of capital.

16-7. a.

	0—1—2—3—4—5—6—7—8—9	
Investment	$(40,000)	
Annual cash flow	$8,000 per year	
Salvage value		$5,000
	4.9464 *(Table 6-3 9 period row, 14% column)*	0.3075 *(Table 6-2 9 period row, 14% column)*

$(40,000) <— (investment)
39,571 <— (annual cash flow × 4.9464)
1,538 <— (salvage value × 0.3075)
$ 1,109 net present value

b. Profitability index = ($41,109 present value of inflows / $40,000 investment) = **1.03**

c. Internal rate of return (actual rate of return) is slightly more than cost of capital of 14%, because the net present value is positive and the profitability index is greater than 1.0.

d. Payback period = **5 years.**

Investment	$(40,000)
Total return in years 1-5 ($8,000 annual cash flow * 5 years)	40,000

16-9. a. The net present value is positive $2,220 (present value of inflows of $26,220 less the investment of $24,000). Therefore, the return on investment is greater than 20%.

b. The payback period should not carry much weight at all, because it does not recognize the time value of money.

16-11.

Proposal	*Investment*	*Net PV*	*PV of Inflows (Investment + Net PV)*	*Profitability Index (PV of Inflows / Outflows)*
1	$50,000	$30,000	$80,000	$80,000 / $50,000 = **1.6**
2	60,000	24,000	84,000	84,000 / 60,000 = **1.4**
3	30,000	15,000	45,000	45,000 / 30,000 = **1.5**
4	45,000	9,000	54,000	54,000 / 45,000 = **1.2**

Proposal 1 is most desirable because its Profitability Index is the highest.

16-13. a.

$$\text{Accounting rate of return} = \frac{\text{Net income}}{\text{Average investment}} = \frac{\$29{,}000 - \$10{,}000\ \#}{(\$100{,}000 + \$90{,}000\ \#\#) / 2} = \mathbf{20\%}$$

\# Depreciation expense = (Cost – Salvage) / Life
= ($80,000 – $50,000) / 3 = $10,000

\## Investment at end of the year = Investment at beginning of the year – Accumulated depreciation
= $100,000 – $10,000 = $90,000

16-13. b. ***Investment:***

		Year 1	*Year 2*	*Year 3*	*Year 4*
Machine	$(80,000)				
Working Capital	(20,000)				
Cash returns:					
Operations		$14,000	$24,000	$29,000	$20,000
Salvage					50,000
Working Capital					20,000
Totals	$(100,000)	$14,000	$24,000	$29,000	$90,000
PV Factor for 18%		0.8475	0.7182	0.6086	0.5158
Present value		$11,865	$17,237	$17,649	$46,422
Sum of present values	93,173 <—				
Net present value	**$ (6,827)**				

Based on this analysis, the investment would *not* be made because the net present value is negative, indicating that the ROI on the project is less than the discount rate of 18%.

c. The net present value analytical approach is the best technique to use because it recognizes the time value of money.